CW00541439

# Al-Isra' wa Al-Mi'raj

Ismail Adam Patel

Al-Aqsa Publishers

Al-Aqsa Publishers
PO Box 5127
Leicester, LE2 0WU, United Kingdom

British Library Cataloguing in Publication Data
A catalogue record for this book is available from the British Library


ISBN 0 9536530 6 4

*Typeset by:* N.A.Qaddoura & Shoayb Adam
*Calligraphy:* Shaykh Suleman Desai

# Contents

# 1 | Introduction

THE NIGHT JOURNEY (al-Isra') of Prophet Muhammad ﷺ from Makkah to Jerusalem and the subsequent Heavenly Ascent (al-Mi'raj) was one of the most incredible and fantastic events in the history of humanity. This journey represented both a turning point in the prophethood and challenged conventional science.

Allah ﷻ with His Might and Majesty folded time and space into one plane and took the Prophet ﷺ through it while the time on Earth stood still. The Prophet ﷺ then journeyed the earth whilst mounted on the Buraq, a horse-like creature capable of travelling cosmic distances in short periods of time. The Prophet ﷺ journeyed through space, and again time stood still. He witnessed heaven and hell, and saw the future and past, experiencing phenomena beyond anything of this world. While such events are undoubtedly beyond scientific comprehension, for Allah ﷻ, the Creator of the universe and of time itself, this was His will and He made it happen through His power.

Any author attempting to recount the story of the Prophet ﷺ and this journey faces the task of organising a chronology for events which transcended different space-time continuums. This may be one of the reasons why the ahadith (Prophetic traditions) on the topic, are difficult to organise. To ease understanding, the incidents are narrated here in a 'linear space' (chronological) order to help facilitate a better understanding and appreciation of the journey from our earthly perspective. This will begin with the Prophet's ﷺ life in Makkah prior to al-Isra'; the journey from Makkah to

Jerusalem; Jerusalem to the heavens; to the extraordinary experiences and events encountered therein; followed by the return journey to Jerusalem; and back to Makkah.

However, it is imperative to be impartial about the sequence of events and be aware that this could have varied with almost all the permutations possible. Nevertheless, this does not distract from the paramount importance, as is almost always the case with the *sirah* or Prophetic biography, of the lessons we derive from the event. No doubt future generations with a more advanced knowledge of space and time will be in a better position to explain al-Isra' and al-Mi'raj in scientific terms, just as we have been better placed today than the preceding generations in understanding Prophet Sulayman 🕮 and his ability to travel in the air.

Imam Ibn Kathir (Allah have mercy on him) in his *tafsir* (Qur'anic exegesis), after meticulous research, has mentioned the names of twenty-five Sahabah (Companions of the Prophet) from whom al-Isra' and al-Mi'raj is reported. Their names are:

'Umar ibn al-Khattab 🕮, 'Ali 🕮, 'Abdullah ibn Mas'ud 🕮, Abu Dharr al-Ghifari 🕮, Malik ibn Sa'sa'ah 🕮, Abu Hurayrah 🕮, Abu Sa'id al-Khudri 🕮, 'Abdullah ibn 'Abbas 🕮, Shaddad ibn Aws 🕮, Ubayy ibn Ka'b 🕮, 'Abd al-Rahman ibn al-Qarat 🕮, Abu Habbah al-Ansari 🕮, Abu Layla 🕮, 'Abdullah ibn 'Amar 🕮, Jabir ibn 'Abdullah 🕮, Hudhayfah ibn Yaman 🕮, Buraydah 🕮, Abu Ayyub al-Ansari 🕮, Abu Umamah 🕮, Samurah ibn Jundub 🕮, Abul Hamra' 🕮, Suhayb al-Rumi 🕮, Umm Hani' 🕮, 'A'ishah 🕮 and Asma' 🕮 bint Abu Bakr.

Ibn Kathir states, "As for the report of al-Isra', all Muslims unananimously concur upon it and only heretics and atheists have denied it."

The ahadith vary in the extent of detail they provide about al-Isra', with most narrating only a part of the journey. However, the framework and structure remains the same throughout all the narrations. This is mainly because the narrations are a response to specific queries and the Companion would only narrate the aspect of al-Isra' and al-Mi'raj he or she has been asked about. Al-Isra' has been questioned by some to undermine Islam by casting doubt on whether such an incident is humanly possible. The central objections lie in the physical nature of the journey and also in the affirmation of life after death attested to by the first-hand experience and account of the Prophet 鑑.

By acknowledging the journey the believer (mu'min) testifies to the will and limitless power of the Almighty, making firm their faith in Him. As for recognising the experience of the Prophet 鑑 in al-Mi'raj, one testifies to the life of the hereafter and the Day of Judgement.

Al-Isra' and al-Mi'raj, therefore, holds fast the faith of a person and consolidates the very central tenet of Islamic teaching - that we are here for a temporary period; created by the Lord, whose powers are limitless; and after death we will be resurrected and judged according to our deeds.

The greatness of al-Isra' thus goes beyond the narrow confines of breaking physical barriers and transcends into believing that the Creator is "He, Allah the One and Only; He is the Eternal and Absolute, He begets none, nor is He begotten, and there is nothing that could be compared to Him."; and thus facilitates one's submission to the greatness of the Lord.

For the successful completion of this project I am indebted to my Creator, whose Bounties and Mercies I cannot begin to enumerate. I am particularly grateful to Shafik Mandhai, Rajnaara Akhtar, Mokrane Guezzou, Ibrahim Hewitt and Shoayb Adam. There have been many others who have encouraged me and to all I am grateful.

# 2 | Circumstances Prior to al-Isra'

FROM THE TIME the Prophet ﷺ received the first revelation in 610AD the Makkans began their hostility and persecution. By 622, towards the end of the Makkan period, Prophet Muhammad's ﷺ hardships were increasing exponentially. Compounding this were the deaths of his beloved wife Khadijah ؓ, who was his confidante and source of emotional support; and in the following month his uncle, Abu Talib who was his protector. Furthermore, his clan Banu Hashim and his Muslim followers were recovering from a boycott imposed by the powerful Quraysh clan that lasted three years. Under this strain, the Prophet ﷺ sought out protection and went to the neighbouring town of Ta'if. Unfortunately the torment and abuse he ﷺ was to suffer there was unparalleled. Hence, this year of his life is known as the 'year of grief and mourning' in the *sirah* of the Prophet ﷺ.

In Ta'if the leaders not only rejected the message but also ordered the people of the town to stone and humiliate Prophet Muhammad ﷺ. The time leading up to al-Isra' was without a doubt the most difficult, lonely and severe period in his earthly existence.

Many years later when his wife 'A'ishah ؓ asked him about his hardship he recalled this period: "'A'ishah ؓ asked the Prophet ﷺ, "Have you seen a day worse than the day of the Battle of Uhud?" The Prophet ﷺ replied, "I have suffered from your people all of what

I suffered. The hardest time that I suffered from them was the day of 'Aqabah[1], when I presented myself to (i.e. invited to Islam) Ibn 'Abd Yalil ibn 'Abd Kulal.[2] He did not accept me. So, I went with deep sorrow and was almost unconscious, until I found myself in Qarn al-Tha'alib. I raised my face and I saw a cloud above me, and I found Jibra'il in it. He called me and said, 'Allah has heard your people's speech to you and what they answered you. He has sent you the Angel of the Mountains; you may order him of whatever you want.' The Angel of the Mountains called me, greeted me, and said, 'O Muhammad, if you would like, I would collapse *Akhshabayn*[3] over them.' The Prophet ﷺ said, 'Nay, I hope that Allah will bring from them those who would worship Allah alone without associating any partners with Him.'"

After the humiliation suffered by Prophet Muhammad ﷺ in Ta'if, he made a very powerful supplication to Allah ﷻ, which reflects both the great magnanimity and deep sorrow of the Prophet ﷺ. His supplication was:

"O Lord, I complain to You of the feebleness of my strength, the scantiness of my resources and the ease with which people humiliate me. O Most Merciful of the merciful, You are the Lord of the oppressed, and You are my Lord. To whom do You entrust me? To a distant one who glowers at me? Or to an enemy to whom You have given power over me? If You are not angry with me, I do not care, but Your strength is more generous for me. I seek refuge in the light of Your countenance for which the darkness becomes radiant, and through which the affairs of this world and the next become good, that You may not be angry with me or Your wrath descend on me. You have the right to blame me until You are satisfied, and there is no power or might except in You."

Besides the torment, humiliation and torture, his concerns now turned towards the difficult return journey to Makkah. The nature of Arabian tribal society was such that any individual coming into a town or a village needed to have an alliance with, or protection from, a man of good standing in that town or village.[4] However, with no protectorate in Makkah and with Ta'if having rejected him, his worries multiplied. Before he entered Makkah he sent messages to a few people seeking protection but to no avail. Finally al-Mutim ibn Adiy, who was a non-believer, offered his protection, which the Prophet ﷺ accepted. Having to seek the protection of a non-Muslim exposes the vulnerability the Prophet ﷺ faced in Makkah.

The loss of his wife and uncle, the distressful journey to Ta'if and his vulnerable position in Makkah, all resulted in this being the most hazardous and distressing time in the Prophet's ﷺ life. It was in this phase of his life that Allah ﷻ took him on al-Isra' and al-Mi'raj, as if to reassure, remind and empower him.

The journey draws attention to the towering and lofty position that the Prophet ﷺ held regardless of the rejection he was facing from his people on the earth. By bringing the Prophet ﷺ to His presence, and showing him ﷺ the world of the hereafter, Allah ﷻ fortified him with a resolute conviction. The Prophet ﷺ was then capable of putting in perspective the trials and tribulations he was encountering on earth. The grandeur that he experienced on the journey washed away the concerns he had for himself, and his sorrow at losing his nearest and dearest. It also made clear the insignificance of those who challenged and questioned the message, and reassured him of the pivotal role and position of his Ummah (Community). Thus the greatness of al-Isra' and al-Mi'raj emerges from the historical context that the Prophet ﷺ found himself in, his position therein, and the impact it had on him as an individual.

# 3 | The Date of al-Isra'

WHILST THE EXACT date of al-Isra' remains unconfirmed as no consensus has ever been reached, the majority of scholars are of the opinion that it took place during the night of 27th Rajab, two years before the emigration (*Hijrah*) of the Prophet ﷺ to Madinah. Allocating a specific date for this event, however, has been difficult simply because it was not mentioned by Prophet Muhammad ﷺ himself or by any of his Companions.

Abdallah Marouf Omar in his PhD thesis on Islamic Jerusalem dedicated a chapter on the significance of the timing of al-Isra'. He suggests that "the entire Prophethood of Muhammad ﷺ lasted for about 22 years and 6 months in the lunar calendar. Half of this period is 11 years and 3 months. If this period is to be counted from the start of the Prophethood, then the middle of his Prophethood would fall in *DhulHijjah* 2 BH. This means that the Night Journey took place almost in the middle or slightly before the middle of Muhammad's ﷺ Prophethood. Ahmad Ismail Nofal argues that the Night Journey took place in the heart of Prophet Muhammad's Prophethood, which agrees with chapter 17 (*al-Isra'*) of the Qur'an that speaks about the Night Journey. This chapter in the Qur'an is at the end of the 1st half of the Qur'an, since it represents the start of the 15th *juz'* (section), out of the 30 *ajz'* (sections) of the Qur'an. This means that the exact middle point of the Qur'an with regard to the *ajz'* would be the end of the 15th *juz'*, which is in chapter 18, namely, *al-Kahf*. It is interesting to note that the middle point of the Qur'an is in chapter 18, directly after chapter 17 of *al-Isra'*. This means that chapter 17, comes slightly before the middle of the Qur'an, which corresponds with the time of the event itself in the Prophethood era."[5]

Imam al-Qurtubi in his tafsir records various opinions on the possible date of al-Isra' and al-Mi'raj. According to Musa ibn 'Uqbah ﷺ, this event came to pass six months before the Hijrah to Madinah. 'A'ishah ﷺ says that Khadijah ﷺ Mother of the Faithful (Umm al-Mu'minin), had passed away before the *salah* or prayer was made obligatory (fard). Imam Zuhri says that the sad demise of Khadijah ﷺ took place seven years after the call to the mission of Prophethood.

In short, renowned and respected scholars of Islam, in the absence of clear ahadith, have not made the specifying of a date for al-Isra' and al-Mi'raj a point of contention. They have, rather, placed an emphasis on understanding the greatness of the journey, the impact it had on the Messenger of Allah ﷺ and the lessons it provides for humanity.

# 4 | The Qur'an

ONE OF THE most incredible events during the auspicious life of Prophet Muhammad ﷺ is undoubtedly his Night Journey from Makkah to Jerusalem and thereafter al-Mi'raj, the ascent to the Sublime Throne. An incredible and miraculous journey, it marks the reality that the Limitless Lord of the Worlds made possible for His servant, Prophet Muhammad ﷺ who was sent to all mankind.

Sadly, despite the *sahih* ahadith relating to the event, some have questioned its authenticity and seeds of doubt are being sown into the hearts of some Muslims. This is not a modern phenomenon, however, but stems from the time that Prophet Muhammad ﷺ announced his experience to the people of Makkah. Nevertheless, despite their rejection, and that of their modern-day counterparts, this incident confirmed to many others the limitless power of the Almighty, and these Muslims surrendered themselves 'utterly' to the Creator, and thus the event made them become more cognisant of Him ﷻ.

There is irrefutable evidence that al-Isra' was a physical journey, in body and spirit, experienced by Prophet Muhammad ﷺ and therein lies its greatness. The early hadith literature has been preserved pristinely by the jurists (fuqaha'), who have sifted the evidence painstakingly to dispel the slightest possibility of innovation or addition to the original account as related by the Prophet ﷺ and transmitted by his Companions—a fact agreed upon by the majority of Islamic scholars.

For Muslims the fact that the Qur'an narrates the episode is sufficient evidence. However, the Qur'an itself enjoins people to apply rigorous thought and research and not take information blindly.

سُبْحَـٰنَ ٱلَّذِىٓ أَسْرَىٰ بِعَبْدِهِۦ لَيْلًا مِّنَ ٱلْمَسْجِدِ ٱلْحَرَامِ إِلَى ٱلْمَسْجِدِ ٱلْأَقْصَا ٱلَّذِى بَـٰرَكْنَا حَوْلَهُۥ لِنُرِيَهُۥ مِنْ ءَايَـٰتِنَآ إِنَّهُۥ هُوَ ٱلسَّمِيعُ ٱلْبَصِيرُ ۞

*Limitless (1) in His glory is He who transported His servant (2) by night from the Sacred Masjid (3) (in Makkah) to the Masjid al-Aqsa (in Jerusalem) – whose surroundings We have blessed (4) – so that We might show him some of Our signs (5). Indeed He alone is the One who hears all and sees all*

(Al-Isra' 17:1)

## 1. Limitless

By introducing the verse with the words "Limitless in His glory" there is an indication of the gravity and magnanimity of the message that is to follow. The attribute of the Lord being "Limitless" dispels any doubts about the pending message even though it may challenge the understanding of reality that humans have. This distinct and, at the same time, compassionate style of the Qur'an simplifies for the reciter understanding and acceptance of the message. It is through the mercy of the Almighty ﷻ that He has made the Qur'an easy to follow for those with understanding minds. There is also a second aspect of "Limitless" that one is alerted to. The verse continues that the object of the journey was to "show him some of Our signs". Hence, not only was the journey out of the ordinary but what the Prophet ﷺ saw and reported was also inconceivable. Seeing these "Limitless" signs of Allah ﷻ at first hand had a profound effect upon the Prophet ﷺ, through which Muslims can derive important lessons and a better understanding of the Creator.

After Allah ﷻ announces that His glory is "Limitless", He informs us that He "transported" His servant by night from

Makkah to Jerusalem. Hence after having been introduced to the power of Allah ﷻ, nobody should have any doubt regarding Him taking His servant on this journey by night. Although the Qur'an does not detail how this was done, we learn from the ahadith that the Prophet Muhammad ﷺ was taken by a celestial creature, smaller than a horse and larger than a mule, called 'Buraq'. Needless to say, therefore, that the transportation was a physical journey and not an apparition or a dream.

## 2. Servant
Even after having undertaken such an extraordinary journey, Allah ﷻ refers to Prophet Muhammad ﷺ as a "servant". This is perhaps to warn the believers not to conflate the rank of Prophethood with that of godhood, which the followers of 'Isa ﷺ have done. The word "servant" has been used several times in the Qur'an to refer to the Prophet ﷺ, *If you are in doubt as to what We have revealed to Our servant...* (Al-Baqarah 2:23); *So did Allah convey the inspiration to His slave* (Al-Najm 53:10) *And when the servant of Allah stood up in prayer...* (Al-Jinn 72:19).

The highest rank of servanthood is epitomized by the Prophet ﷺ someone who experienced this unprecedented journey not through his own ability but that of the Limitless Lord of the worlds. Hence the Prophet ﷺ fulfils the role of someone who labours and exerts himself for the benefit of another, but is a special beneficiary of the Lord. The supreme rank of Prophet Muhammad ﷺ is unmatched, and made all the more pertinent by being a servant of Allah ﷻ.

## 3. Masjid
It is of significance that al-Isra' took place before the Hijrah, when Makkah and the Ka'bah were in the hands of pagans and Jerusalem and Masjid al-Aqsa were controlled by the Persians. Idols were placed in and around the Ka'bah and Masjid al-Aqsa was used as a garbage dump and yet, despite the Ka'bah being a place of spiritual impurity and al-Aqsa one of physical impurity, Allah ﷻ, the

All-Knowing, the Creator, mentions both places by name in the first verse of the Qur'an chapter (Surah) called al-Isra' to honour them, and calls them both His 'Masjid'.

This is a clear indication that despite episodes in history where these two holy sites have been neglected, to Allah ﷻ they have always been, and will always be, His honoured Masajid (plural of Masjid, a place of prostration in prayer). It is thus up to those who claim to follow the commands of Allah ﷻ to ensure that they remain pure and visited by those exalting Him. A failure to ensure the purity of these sites is a colossal loss on the part of the believers, one which brings repercussions for the whole Ummah in this world and the hereafter.

The second aspect regarding the concept of "Masjid" is that it does not have to be a physical building, for it can be deduced from this verse that any land which Allah ﷻ has blessed, with or without any buildings, can be regarded as a Masjid. This is borne out by the historical fact that when al-Isra' and al-Mi'raj took place, there were no complete buildings within the Noble Sanctuary of al-Aqsa; the only building present was the surrounding wall and perhaps a few ruins. As the following hadith from *Sahih al-Bukhari* verifies, the Prophet ﷺ described the *city* of Jerusalem (Bayt al-Maqdis) and not any particular building within, which also validated Prophet Muhammad's narrative ﷺ of al-Isra', and the authenticity of his Prophethood: Jabir ibn 'Abdullah ﷺ relates that the Prophet ﷺ said:

> "When the people of Quraysh did not believe me (i.e. the story of his Night Journey), I stood up in the Hijr[1] and Allah ﷻ displayed Jerusalem in front of me, and I began describing it to them while I was looking at it."

Further proof of this was presented, if any was needed, when 'Umar ﷺ entered al-Aqsa Sanctuary and he was greatly perturbed at the appalling state of the place. He said, "O people, do what I am doing"; kneeling down in the midst of the rubbish, he gathered it by the handful into the lower part of his mantle.[2] The Companions followed suit and worked throughout the day until all the rubbish accumulated by the Byzantines was cleared. Thereafter he called for Ka'b ﷺ and asked, "Where do you think we should establish the place of prayer (the masjid)?" Ka'b ﷺ said, "Place the Masjid behind the Rock." 'Umar ﷺ disagreed as this would mean people having to stand behind the rock in order to face the qibla[3] and he feared people might begin venerating it.[4] Thus 'Umar ﷺ built the Masjid with its qibla in front of the rock. 'Umar ﷺ then ordered the construction of a Masjid where today's elegant black-domed Masjid, commonly called Masjid al-Aqsa, stands.

The first request 'Umar ﷺ made upon entering Jerusalem was to be taken to the precinct of al-Aqsa. This is not surprising, not only because this was the station between al-Isra' and al-Mi'raj but also because the significance of al-Aqsa for Muslims begins with Prophet Adam ﷺ and continues through to Prophet Dawud (David) ﷺ. Prophet Dawud ﷺ united the scattered tribes of Israel and captured Jerusalem. Prophet Sulayman (Soloman) ﷺ, his son, inherited the kingdom and built a place of worship on the hills of Moriah. After Prophet Sulayman's death the kingdom split into two parts, Israel in the north and Judah (including Jerusalem) in the south. After 200 years of rivalry, Israel was conquered by a ruler from the Levant (al-Sham).

The temple built by Prophet Sulayman ﷺ was gradually despoiled and the pure teachings of Prophet Musa (Moses) ﷺ were corrupted. In 586 BCE Nebuchadnezzar captured Jerusalem and razed the whole temple to the ground. Fifty years later, the Persians captured Jerusalem and allowed the reconstruction of the second temple. Around 300 BCE the Greeks captured Jerusalem and dedicated the temple to Zeus. By 164 BCE the Hasmonean Jews had taken control of the temple and ruled over it for a century. When, in 63 BCE, Herod was appointed King of Judea he slaughtered the Hasmoneans and claimed guardianship of the temple. A period of oppression and barbarism followed and it was in this period that Prophet 'Isa (Jesus) ﷺ was born. His mission was to bring the people back to the teachings of Prophets Ibrahim 🕊 and Musa 🕊.

After ʿIsa 🕊, years of riots and massacres ensued over control of the temple. The Roman emperor Titus captured Jerusalem in 70 AD and reduced the temple to rubble. A new city named Aelia was built on the ruins of the city with a temple dedicated to Jupiter.

In the early part of the 4th Century the Roman emperor Constantine became a Christian and many Churches were built in Jerusalem. For a short period in 620 AD the Persians captured Jerusalem and massacred the Christians. The temple still remained in ruins for hundreds of years and was used as a rubbish tip. The Jews were banished from Jerusalem for nearly 600 years (apart from the few years of Persian rule) but were given renewed access under Islamic rule.

Muslims consider al-Aqsa to have been built first by Prophet Adam 🕊. Reference is drawn from the hadith in *Sahih al-Bukhari*,

> Abū Dharr 🕊 reported that he asked the Prophet 🕊, "O Prophet of Allah, which Masjid was built first on earth?" The Prophet 🕊 replied, "The Sacred Masjid of Makkah." Abū Dharr again asked, "Which was next?" The Prophet 🕊 said, "The Masjid al-Aqṣā." "How long was the period between them?" Abū Dharr asked. The Prophet 🕊 said, "Forty years. Apart from these, offer your prayers anywhere when it is time to pray, although excellence is in praying in these Masajid."

Imam al-Qurtubi (Allah have mercy on him) says, "There are different opinions regarding the construction of Masjid al-Aqsa. Some assert that Adam 🕊 established Masjid al-Haram in Makkah and then proceeded to build Masjid al-Aqsa forty years later. Others assert the angels laid the foundation of Masjid al-Haram and after forty years established Masjid al-Aqsa. There are a lot of possibilities and Allah knows best."[5]

Ibn Hajar al-ʿAsqalani (Allah have mercy on him) says, "The first to establish the foundation of Masjid al-Aqsa was Adam 🕊, some say angels, some say Nuh (Noah) 🕊 and some say Dawud 🕊 and I incline towards those who say that Adam ☉ was the first to lay the foundation of Masjid al-Aqsa."⁶

## 4. Blessed

We are further informed that Allah ☉ has designated Masjid al-Aqsa and its surrounding area as "blessed". The "blessed land" under the Islamic ethos means land associated with *barakah* — the land over which Allah ☉ has endowed spiritual and physical blessings from which all of humanity and Allah's creation can derive benefit. This *barakah* also extends to the people residing within this land, on the condition that they abide by the commands of Allah ☉ and more specifically, that they practise Islam.

Al-Aqsa has been honoured and glorified by Allah ☉ and showered with His divine blessings for the benefit, enlightenment and guidance of all mankind. The Qur'an states that the blessings of this land are for "al-'Alamin", meaning for "the whole world's creation" until eternity. It implies that the blessings are not restricted to any specific group of people or species but encompass all living and non-living things.

The boundary of this "blessed land" is not clear and there are differences of opinion about its exact extent. Some classical Islamic scholars of the Qur'an and Sunnah - including Ibn Kathir, Imam al-Qurtubi and Ibn al-Jawzi (Allah have mercy on them all) - consider the whole area of al-Sham (modern-day Lebanon, Syria, Jordan and Palestine) as blessed. Other interpreters believe that the blessed land is contiguous from the Hijaz (Saudi Arabia) through al-Sham to Egypt. A further, and maybe a more logical opinion, is that within the area of the modern Middle East there are pockets of "blessed land" like the compound of al-Aqsa, the Prophet's Masjid ☉ in Madinah, and the Holy Masjid in Makkah. However, in all the opinions on the extent of the "blessed land", al-Aqsa is included.

The blessings of al-Aqsa in particular and al-Sham in general have been further expounded in the Holy Qur'an and the traditions of Prophet Muhammad ☉.

a. After Musa ﷺ took the Children of Israel away from the tyranny of the Pharoah in Egypt to the outskirts of Palestine, he directed them to enter the "Holy Land". The Holy Land described in the Qur'an is the land of Palestine in general and the city of Jerusalem in particular.

$$يَٰقَوْمِ ٱدْخُلُوا۟ ٱلْأَرْضَ ٱلْمُقَدَّسَةَ ٱلَّتِى كَتَبَ ٱللَّهُ لَكُمْ وَلَا تَرْتَدُّوا۟ عَلَىٰٓ أَدْبَارِكُمْ فَتَنقَلِبُوا۟ خَٰسِرِينَ ۝$$

*My people! Enter the Holy Land which Allah has assigned for you, and do not turn back for then you will turn about losers.*

(Al-Ma'idah 5:21)

It is significant to note that the Qur'an refers to the land of Palestine as "holy" and not as a "promised" land, a clear indication of the all-encompassing nature of Allah ﷻ who bestows favours on the whole of mankind rather than a specific group. It cannot be befitting for the Creator of mankind to favour one group over any other by the simple virtue of their birth, for as the Creator Himself informs us, the nearest to Him are those who are most pious, that is those who abide by His commands.

b. In Surah al-A'raf, Allah ﷻ further informs us that He poured His blessings on to the land both east and west of Jerusalem. The verse below refers to the time when Jerusalem was the abode of the children of Israel (the name given to the descendents of Prophet Yaqoub – Jacob – ﷺ also known as Israel), and is probably referring to the era of Prophet Sulayman ﷺ.

$$وَأَوْرَثْنَا ٱلْقَوْمَ ٱلَّذِينَ كَانُوا۟ يُسْتَضْعَفُونَ مَشَٰرِقَ ٱلْأَرْضِ وَمَغَٰرِبَهَا ٱلَّتِى بَٰرَكْنَا فِيهَا ۖ وَتَمَّتْ كَلِمَتُ رَبِّكَ ٱلْحُسْنَىٰ عَلَىٰ بَنِىٓ إِسْرَٰٓئِيلَ بِمَا صَبَرُوا۟ ۖ وَدَمَّرْنَا مَا كَانَ يَصْنَعُ فِرْعَوْنُ وَقَوْمُهُۥ وَمَا كَانُوا۟ يَعْرِشُونَ ۝$$

*And We made a people, considered weak (and of no account), inheritors of lands in both east and west – lands where We sent down Our blessings. The fair promise of your Lord was fulfilled for the children of Israel, because they had patience and constancy, and We levelled to the ground the great works and fine buildings which Pharaoh and his people erected (with such pride).*

(Al-A'raf 7:137)

The land of Palestine was under the rule of the Egyptian Pharaoh; hence the reference to the levelling to the ground of the great buildings which the Pharaoh erected.

c. Prophet Ibrahim ﷺ and his immediate family were deported by his clansmen from the city of his birth, Ur, in a country called Sumer (present-day Iraq), for preaching the Oneness (Tawhid) of Allah ﷻ. The Qur'an informs us that Ibrahim ﷺ was delivered by Allah ﷻ to the land, which Allah ﷻ has "blessed for the nations". This land, which Allah ﷻ eloquently refers to as "blessed for the nations", is the glorious land of Palestine. Prophet Ibrahim ﷺ is believed to have re-constructed Masjid al-Aqsa in Jerusalem with his son Ishaq (Isaac) ﷺ.

وَنَجَّيْنَٰهُ وَلُوطًا إِلَى ٱلْأَرْضِ ٱلَّتِي بَٰرَكْنَا فِيهَا لِلْعَٰلَمِينَ ٧١

*But We delivered him (Ibrahim) and (his nephew) Lut (and directed them) to the land which We have blessed for the nations.*

(Al-Anbiya' 21:71)

d. The kingdom of Prophet Sulayman ﷺ was in present-day Palestine, with al-Quds (Jerusalem) as its capital. The Qur'an refers to the whole area where Prophet Sulayman ﷺ travelled as "the land which We had blessed".

وَلِسُلَيْمَٰنَ ٱلرِّيحَ عَاصِفَةً تَجْرِي بِأَمْرِهِۦٓ إِلَى ٱلْأَرْضِ ٱلَّتِي بَٰرَكْنَا فِيهَا وَكُنَّا بِكُلِّ شَيْءٍ عَٰلِمِينَ ٨١

*(It was Our power that made) the violent (unruly) wind flow (tamely) for Sulayman, to his order, to the land which We had blessed, for We do know all things.*

(Al-Anbiya' 21:81)

e. In Surah Saba', there is a reference to the people of Saba' in Yemen who frequented the frankincense highway via Arabia to Syria in the north and Egypt to the west. The "cities on which We had poured Our blessings" refers to the cities of al-Sham including al-Quds (Jerusalem).

وَجَعَلْنَا بَيْنَهُمْ وَبَيْنَ ٱلْقُرَى ٱلَّتِى بَـٰرَكْنَا فِيهَا قُرًى ظَـٰهِرَةً وَقَدَّرْنَا فِيهَا ٱلسَّيْرَ سِيرُواْ فِيهَا لَيَالِىَ وَأَيَّامًا ءَامِنِينَ ۝

*Between them and the cities on which We had poured Our blessings, We had placed cities in prominent positions, and between them We had appointed stages of journey in due proportion. Travel therein, secure, by night and by day.*

(Saba' 34:18)

The verses of the Holy Qur'an indicate that unlike any other place on earth, Allah ﷻ has blessed the land of Palestine. Allah ﷻ blessed and honoured this area prior to any event or incident through His great mercy, and the events that have taken place there are further reasons for the faithful to build their love and affection for this area. There is no doubt that the presence of so many Prophets and the historical link to them builds a bond but it is Allah ﷻ through His great mercy and wisdom, who has chosen the area around al-Aqsa to be blessed.

Zuhayr ibn Muhammad ؓ reports Prophet Muhammad ﷺ to have said, "Allah ﷻ has blessed what lies between al-Arish (in Egypt) and the Euphrates and has made Palestine particularly holy."

[Kanz al-'Umal]

Zayd ibn Thabit ﷺ reports that the Prophet ﷺ said, "How blessed is al-Sham!" The Companions around asked, "Why is that?" The Messenger ﷺ replied, "I see the angels of Allah ﷺ spread their wings over al-Sham." Ibn 'Abbas ﷺ added, "and the Prophets lived in it. There is not a single inch in al-Quds (Jerusalem) where a Prophet has not prayed or an angel not stood."

[Tirmidhi and Imam Ahmad]

'Abdullah ibn 'Umar ﷺ reports that the Prophet ﷺ said, "O Allah! Bestow Your blessings on our Sham! O Allah! Bestow Your blessings on our Yemen." The people said, "And also on our Najd[7]." He said, "O Allah! Bestow Your blessings on our Sham! O Allah! Bestow Your blessings on our Yemen." The people said, "O Messenger of Allah! And also on our Najd." I think the third time the Prophet ﷺ said, "There (in Najd) is the place of earthquakes and afflictions and from there shall appear the horn of the Devil."

[Sahih al-Bukhari]

Prophet Muhammad ﷺ prayed for the blessing of the people of al-Sham. Anas ibn Malik ﷺ reports that the Prophet ﷺ looked towards Iraq, al-Sham and Yemen then said, "O Allah! Bring their hearts over to Your obedience and relieve them of their burdens."

[Tirmidhi]

Once, the Prophet ﷺ advised 'Abdullah ibn Hawwala ﷺ to join the army in al-Sham, over any other. However, after noticing Ibn Hawwala's indifference the Prophet ﷺ said, "Do you know what Allah says about al-Sham? Allah says, "Al-Sham you are the quintessence of My lands (*safwati min biladi*) and I shall inhabit you with the chosen ones among My servants."

[Al-Tabarani]

## 5. Show him some of Our Signs

The term "show him" is very significant as it emphasizes that Prophet Muhammad ﷺ was physically taken to see some of the signs of Allah ﷻ. If this was a dream the Qur'an would not have said "We showed him some of Our Signs", and it would have also been superfluous for the Makkans and others to disagree, since in a dream one can imagine boundless events and encounter fantastic experiences. The Qur'an reiterates this point with emphasis:

$$\text{لَقَدۡ رَأَىٰ مِنۡ ءَايَـٰتِ رَبِّهِ ٱلۡكُبۡرَىٰٓ ۝}$$

*Indeed he did see of the greatest signs of his Lord.*

(Al-Najm 53:18)

$$\text{وَإِذۡ قُلۡنَا لَكَ إِنَّ رَبَّكَ أَحَاطَ بِٱلنَّاسِ ۚ وَمَا جَعَلۡنَا ٱلرُّءۡيَا ٱلَّتِىٓ أَرَيۡنَـٰكَ إِلَّا فِتۡنَةً لِّلنَّاسِ}$$
$$\text{وَٱلشَّجَرَةَ ٱلۡمَلۡعُونَةَ فِى ٱلۡقُرۡءَانِ ۚ وَنُخَوِّفُهُمۡ فَمَا يَزِيدُهُمۡ إِلَّا طُغۡيَـٰنًا كَبِيرًا ۝}$$

*We said to you that your Lord encompasses all mankind. We have the vision which We have shown you, as also the tree cursed in this Qur'an, only a trial for people. We seek to put fear in their hearts, but it only increases their gross transgression.*

(Al-Isra' 17:60)

If this verse is read in isolation without one being aware of the messages preceding and following it, one could easily be misled to believe that Prophet Muhammad ﷺ was shown a vision as in a dream during the night of al-Isra'. But read in its full context one realizes that the warning Allah ﷻ gave is regarding miracles. In an earlier verse it states, "Nothing hinders Us from sending miraculous signs except that the people of former times treated them as false. To the Thamud We gave the she-camel as a sign to open their eyes, but they did wrong in respect of her. We never send signs for any purpose other than to give warning." (17:59)

Ibn Kathir's Quran'ic exegesis clarifies the matter: "Islam has one miracle to prove its truth. That is the Qur'an. It is a book that maps a whole system of life, addressing both mind and heart and meeting all needs of human nature. It remains open to all generations to read and believe in. It is valid for all time. A physical miracle is given to one generation and its effects are limited to those who witness it. Yet the majority of those who witnessed such physical miracles did not believe in them. The example given here is that of the Thamud who were given the miracle they sought. It came in the shape of a she-camel. Yet they transgressed and slaughtered the she-camel. Hence, Allah's warning came to pass and they were destroyed as a result of their denials that continued even after this clear, miraculous sign had been given to them. All such signs were given by way of warning. They heralded the inevitable punishment, a punishment that was bound to be inflicted should rejection of the message continue.

History being such, it was necessary that the final message should not be accompanied by any physical miracle (sent for trial). This message (of Islam) is not meant for one generation; it is addressed to all future generations. It is a message that addresses the human mind with all its receptive faculties. It respects man's intellect and power of understanding.

The preternatural events that took place at the time of Prophet Muhammad ﷺ, or happened to him, such as that of his Night Journey, were not meant as proof of his message but these were given as a test for his people."

Some of those who believed in the message preached by the Prophet ﷺ reverted to unbelief after he told them about his Night Journey. Others, however, became firmer than ever in their belief. Hence, it is true that what Allah ﷻ showed His servant on that night was meant as a "trial for men", so that they would reaffirm their faith. Al-Bukhari recorded that "Ibn 'Abbas said regarding the verse 'We have the vision which We have shown you, as also the tree cursed in this Qur'an', it's only a trial for people, this is the vision the Messenger of Allah ﷺ saw with his own eyes on the night when he was taken on al-Isra."

It becomes clear that the reason al-Isra' is "a trial for people" is because of its exceptional nature and not because the Prophet ﷺ saw all this in his dreams as the detractors would assume.

There is a weak hadith attributed to the Mother of the Faithful 'A'ishah ؓ which states, "The Prophet's sanctified body was not missing on the Night Journey." Besides this hadith being weak, it can be understood that the event of al-Isra' and al-Mi'raj happened so quickly in earthly time that the Prophet ﷺ was not missing. But a few detractors have tried to construe this as meaning 'A'ishah ؓ allegedly reported that the Prophet ﷺ never left in bodily form and therefore this was a spiritual journey. It has to be recalled that when the Prophet ﷺ was taken on al-Isra, he was not married to 'A'isha ؓ and thus not cohabiting with her. However, in another authentic hadith 'A'ishah ؓ reports, "The Prophet ﷺ did not see Almighty Allah with his eye," indicating that she believed that the journey was in both body and soul. Had she thought that it was in soul only, she would not have proposed that the Prophet ﷺ did not see his Lord with his eye.

Hence, the Prophet ﷺ was taken and raised to be shown "some of Our Signs" which included seeing the previous Prophets ﷺ, Masjid al-Aqsa, heaven, hell, the condition of their respective inhabitants and much more.

# 5 | Makkah to Jerusalem

ACCORDING TO IBN Kathir (Allah have mercy on him), twenty-five Sahabah have narrated the incident of al-Isra', with all the narrations being traced back to two Companions (who were the original sources), Abu Dharr ﷺ and Malik ibn Sa'sa'ah ﷺ. All the scholars of hadith have included in their collections the journey of al-Isra'. Imam al-Bukhari in his *Jami' al-sahih,* in the "Book of Tawhid" has a chapter devoted to al-Mi'raj, whilst Imam Muslim's *Jami' al-sahih* has a chapter called "Isra'" in the "Book of the Beginning of the Revelation".

As noted in the introduction, in order to understand al-Isra' and al-Mi'raj within the familiar concepts of linear time frames and three-dimensional space travel, ahadith from several sources have been collated to present this incredible journey in a coherent manner. This poses a danger on the "time/space frame" to some specific incidents along the journey. However, endnotes have been added wherever opinions differ and alternative views are held. Only a portion of ahadith is narrated with corresponding headings to help understand the linear flow of the journey. Full versions of the ahadith are referenced in Appendix 3 for anyone seeking to study them further.

Abu Dharr ﷺ reports that the Messenger ﷺ said, "One night I was asleep, in the Makkan Sacred Precinct (al-Haram) near the Ka'bah when I was woken by Jibra'il. He informed me of the divine will and took me to the well of Zamzam, where upon he opened my chest and poured wisdom and faith into it. Then he sealed it. I was then presented with the beautiful Buraq. This is an animal larger than a mule but smaller than a horse. I mounted it..."[1]

Anas ﷺ narrates: "The Buraq began to strut and Jibra'il said, 'Why are you doing this? By Allah, no one more honoured by Allah has ever ridden you than he.'" He said, "He (the Buraq) started to sweat..."[2]

The root word *Buraq* is derived either from "barq" which means light or "bariq" denoting white, both indicating purity and speed. The Buraq was used by previous Prophets ﷺ and hence we see that Allah ﷻ chose the same mode of transport for the final Prophet ﷺ rather than "whisking" him from Makkah to Madinah without any conveyance, which Allah ﷻ could have done if He so wished.

Jibra'il accompanied the Prophet ﷺ and sat in front on the Buraq and the Prophet ﷺ was behind him. They travelled on the Buraq in this manner until they reached Bayt al-Maqdis (Jerusalem). The Buraq travelled at a tremendous speed, whereby one of its stride traversed the space in sight.

Anas Ibn Malik ﷺ reported that the Messenger of Allah ﷺ said: "He (the Buraq) puts its hoof wherever its eyesight ends." He ﷺ said, "I rode it (and started the journey) until I arrived at Bayt al-Maqdis." He ﷺ continued, "Then I tied it to a ring that the Prophets used to tie their animals on." He ﷺ said, "Then I entered the Masjid, and I prayed two units of prayer, then I went out, so Jibra'il brought me a cup of wine and a cup of milk. I chose the milk, so Jibra'il said, 'You chose the *fitrah* (natural goodness, good instinct),' then we were raised to heaven..."[3]

## Choice of Drink
In the above hadith it is reported that the Prophet ﷺ was offered wine and milk in Bayt al-Maqdis. However, Muslim reports on the authority of Abu Hurayrah ﷺ that these drinks were offered in the heavens, near the Lote-tree of the Farthest Boundary (Sidrat

al Muntaha), and adds that the Prophet ﷺ chose milk. In *Sahih al-Bukhari* it is mentioned that the Prophet ﷺ was in front of the Oft-frequented House[4] (Bayt al-Ma'mur) when he was offered wine, milk and honey in separate containers.

It is possible all the narrations are authentic and correct on the basis that he ﷺ was to drink more than once on this journey. When the Prophet ﷺ took the milk, Jibra'il remarked:

"Had you taken the wine, your Ummah would have certainly gone astray..."[5]

This statement shows that the character and deeds of a leader have a direct impact on his followers.[6]

Abu Hurayrah ﷺ narrates, "On the night the Messenger of Allah ﷺ was taken on the Night Journey, two cups—one containing wine and the other milk—were presented to him at Jerusalem. He looked at them and took the cup of milk. Jibra'il said, 'Praise be to Allah who guided you to the *fitrah;* had you taken (the cup of) wine, your Ummah would have certainly gone astray.'"

[Sahih al-Bukhari]

### Prayer in Masjid al-Aqsa

Anas ibn Malik narrates, "The Prophet ﷺ was offered a drink of water, milk, or wine... Then Adam ﷺ and all the other Prophets ﷺ were resurrected and the Messenger of Allah led them (in prayer) that night."[7]

Ibn Kathir (Allah have mercy on him) narrates a hadith, "Then I left and it was not more than a little while when a lot of people gathered, and someone called for the prayer and the prayer was established." He (the Prophet ﷺ) continued, "So we stood in lines waiting for someone to come and lead us, then Jibra'il took my hand and asked me to lead the prayer, and I did. After the end of the prayer

Jibra'il asked me, 'O Muhammad, do you know who prayed behind you?' I said, 'No'. He said, 'Every Prophet sent by Allah 🕮 prayed behind you.' Then Jibra'il took my hand and we ascended to heaven."

Al-Hasan ibn 'Arafah, narrates "On the way to Masjid al-Aqsa I met 'Isa... then I met Musa... then I met Ibrahim (i.e. before arriving at al-Aqsa). Then we went until we arrived at al-Aqsa Masjid, and I went down and tied the animal (i.e. the Buraq) in the ring that is in the gate of the Masjid where the Prophets used to tie (their animals).

"Then I entered the Masjid and I recognised the Prophets bowing and prostrating, then two cups were brought to me, one was honey and the other was milk, I took the milk and drank, so Jibra'il put his hand on my shoulder and said, 'By the Allah of Muhammad, you chose the *fitrah*.' Then the prayer was established and I led them (i.e. the Prophets)."

Abu Hurayrah 🕮 narrates that the Messenger of Allah 🕮 said: "I was standing in the Hijr while (the tribe of) Quraysh were asking me about my Night Journey, they asked me about things in Bayt al-Maqdis that I was not sure of, so I felt troubled more than I ever felt before." He 🕮 continued, "So Allah 🕮 visualised Bayt al-Maqdis in front of me, and they didn't ask me about anything except that I answered them regarding it. I saw myself in a group of Prophets. Musa 🕮 (who was amongst them) was standing in prayer; a big man with curly hair who resembled one of the (tribesmen of) Shanu'ah. 'Isa 🕮 (Jesus) the son of Maryam (Mary) (upon whom be peace) was also standing in prayer; the closest to him in resemblance is 'Urwah ibn Mas'ud al-Thaqafi. Ibrahim (upon whom be peace) was also standing in prayer; the most closest one to resemble him is your companion (meaning himself). Then the prayer time came, and I led them (in prayer); and when I finished the prayer someone said, 'O Muhammad, this is Malik, hell's gatekeeper, so greet him.' I turned my face towards him, and he greeted me first."[8]

This hadith is clear in saying that Prophet Muhammad ﷺ led all the Prophets ﷺ in prayer. The assembly of the greatest and the congregational prayer of the best of the Creation to grace this world, led by the Greatest of the Creation ﷺ marks the end of the horizontal part of the journey.

When the Prophet ﷺ set out for the heavens, a ladder of extraordinary beauty was lowered before him. According to some narrations, one ladder was of gold and another was of silver, while another narration adds that they were also studded with pearls. As they journeyed upwards by the ladder, the Prophet ﷺ was escorted on his right and left by a procession of angels until they arrived in the heavens and the doors were opened for them.

### The Significance of Praying in al-Aqsa

The fact that the Prophet ﷺ was taken to al-Aqsa prior to the Sublime Throne builds the bond between the first place of worship built on earth and the second, as the hadith below indicates:

> Abu Dharr ﷺ reported that he asked the Prophet ﷺ, "O Messenger of Allah, which Masjid was built first on earth?" The Prophet ﷺ replied, "The Sacred Masjid of Makkah." Abu Dharr again asked, "Which was next?" The Prophet ﷺ said, "The Al-Aqsa Masjid." "How long was the period between them?" Abu Dharr asked. The Prophet ﷺ replied, "Forty years..."
>
> [Sahih al-Bukhari and Sahih Muslim]

The Prophet's praying ﷺ in al-Aqsa consolidates this bond between the first two places of worship built on earth. It also provides al-Aqsa with special significance as this is the only place known to us on earth where all the Prophets of Allah prayed together at one given time led by the final Prophet Muhammad ﷺ. The fact that all the Prophets ﷺ were assembled together in al-Aqsa on this special night indicates the inclusive nature of Islam attested to by the Qur'an ; "Say (O Muslims!), 'We believe in Allah and in that which has been revealed to us; in that which was revealed to Ibrahim, Isma'il, Ishaq,

Ya'qub, and their descendents; in that which was given to Musa and 'Isa; and in that which was given to the Prophets from their Lord'; We do not make any distinction between any of them..." (2:36)

The fact that Prophet Muhammad ﷺ lead all of the other Prophets ﷺ in prayer is a clear indication of his being a leader of all the Prophets ﷺ and therefore a salient call to all humanity and the People of the Book to now come under the guidance of the final Prophet, Muhammad ﷺ.

For Muslims, the prayer by Prophet Muhammad ﷺ in al-Aqsa declares the connection, firstly, between the Ka'bah and al-Aqsa, and secondly, between the Prophet ﷺ (and thereby all Muslims) and al-Aqsa. Leading the Prophets ﷺ in prayer in al-Aqsa further signifies inheriting the legacy of the other Prophets ﷺ, and the leadership of humankind.

It also transpires that Bayt al-Maqdis is the only site known to us where Allah ﷻ sent His revelations in the form of a Book to His Prophets, including Prophet Muhammad ﷺ. It is in al-Aqsa that Allah ﷻ sent revelations to Prophet Ibrahim ﷺ; to Prophet Dawud ﷺ for the Zabur (Psalms); to Prophet 'Isa ﷺ for the Injil (Evangel); and to Prophet Muhammad ﷺ the following Qurani'c verse:[9]

$$\text{وَسْـَٔلْ مَنْ أَرْسَلْنَا مِن قَبْلِكَ مِن رُّسُلِنَآ أَجَعَلْنَا مِن دُونِ ٱلرَّحْمَـٰنِ ءَالِهَةً يُعْبَدُونَ ۝}$$

*And ask the Messengers whom We sent before you, did We appoint any other gods, other than the Most Compassionate (i.e. Allah), that might be worshipped?*

(Al-Zukhruf 43:45)

The importance of all this for Muslims has been reflected in the reward and virtue of praying in al-Aqsa. Ibn al-Jawzi and Abu Bakr al-Wasiti (Allah have mercy on them both) stated that many scholars of Islam believe that it is not only the reward for prayers in al-Haram al-Sharif (al-Aqsa, the Noble Sanctuary) that are multiplied in comparison to prayers elsewhere, but also the rewards for all good deeds therein are multiplied. Similarly, the punishments for bad deeds in this Holy area are also believed to be multiplied.

The psychology behind increasing the reward for virtues is clearly to imbibe within the believers love, affection and a need to incline towards these Holy sites. The increased merits of praying at al-Aqsa are a clear signal for the believers to frequent it and ensure its well-being.

## A. *Virtues of praying*

Abu Darda' ⬥ relates that the Prophet ⬥ said, "A prayer in Makkah is worth 100,000 times; a prayer in my Masjid (in Madinah) is worth 1,000 times; and a prayer in al-Aqsa is worth 500 times more than anywhere else."

[Al-Tabarani, al-Bayhaqi and al-Suyuti]

Anas ibn Malik ⬥ relates that the Prophet ⬥ said, "The prayer of a person in his house is a single prayer; his prayer in the Masjid of his tribe has the reward of twenty-five prayers; his prayer in the Masjid wherein the Friday prayer is observed has the reward of five hundred prayers; his prayer in Masjid al-Aqsa has a reward of five thousand prayers; his prayer in my Masjid (the Prophet's Masjid in Madinah) has a reward of fifty thousand prayers; and the prayer in the Sacred Masjid at Makkah has a reward of one hundred thousand prayers."

[Tirmidhi and Ibn Majah]

## B. *Virtues of performing I'tikaf*

If someone makes a vow to perform i'tikaf (seclusion for worship) in Masjid al-Haram (in Makkah), the Prophet's Masjid (in Madinah), or in Masjid al-Aqsa (in Jerusalem), he is to fulfil his vow, as the Prophet ⬥ said, "One should not undertake journeys except to three Masajid, Masjid al-Haram, Masjid al-Aqsa, or this Masjid (the Prophet's Masjid)."

If someone vows to perform i'tikaf in another Masjid, it is not obligatory on him to fulfil it and he may perform that i'tikaf in any Masjid, for Allah ﷻ did not specify any particular place for His worship, and there is no superiority of one Masjid over another (with the exception of the three Masajid mentioned above). It has been confirmed that the Prophet ﷺ said, "A prayer in my Masjid is superior to one thousand prayers in any other Masjid but Masjid al-Haram (in Makkah), and a prayer in that Masjid is superior to a prayer in my Masjid by one hundred prayers."

> Thus, if someone makes a vow to perform i'tikaf in the Prophet's Masjid, he may fulfil it in Masjid al-Haram since that one is superior to the Prophet's Masjid.
>
> [Fiqh al-Sunnah]

## C. *Virtues of charity*

This hadith is exceptional, as it is the only hadith that draws a parallel between charity and performing *salah* (formal prayer). This should encourage the believers to donate towards al-Haram al-Sharif (al-Aqsa). No other similar recommendation has been made for any of the other Masajid. Muslims are requested directly to oversee the welfare of Masjid al-Aqsa and make this a duty of each and every one. The Prophet's proclamation ﷺ of assisting Masjid al-Aqsa, coupled with the mention of performing *salah* there, should not be underestimated and is a clear indication for the believers to engage in the welfare of al-Haram al-Sharif (al-Aqsa).

> Maymunah bint Sa'd ؓ relates that she asked the Prophet ﷺ, "O Prophet ﷺ! Inform us about Bayt al-Maqdis (Jerusalem)." He said, "Visit it for prayer." She asked, "If one of us cannot visit it, what should we do?" He said, "If you cannot go for prayer then send some oil to be used in its lamps; whosoever gives oil for its lamps, will be as if he has prayed in it."
>
> [Imam Ahmad, Ibn Majah, Sunan Abu Dawud, and al-Tabarani]

This hadith is a clear indication of the high regard for Masjid al-Aqsa that Prophet Muhammad ﷺ wished to emphasize to the Muslims.

### D. *Travelling for prayers*

Yet again, we see the Sacred Law (Shari'ah) teaching and encouraging us to visit al-Haram al-Sharif (al-Aqsa), seeking to build in our hearts love and affection for the blessed place. The encouragement to travel towards al-Aqsa is also a signal to the believers to keep themselves informed about Masjid al-Aqsa, assist with its needs, and increase their *taqwa* (God-conciousness) by building love for Masjid al-Aqsa, one of the greatest symbols of Islam.

Abu Hurayrah ﷺ relates that the Prophet ﷺ said, "You should not undertake a special journey to visit any place other than the three Masajid with the expectations of getting greater reward, the Sacred Masjid of Makkah, this Masjid of mine, and Masjid al-Aqsa (of Jerusalem)." In another narration the words are, "For three Masajid a special journey may be undertaken, the Sacred Masjid (Ka'bah), my Masjid, and the Masjid of al-Quds (Jerusalem)."

[Sahih Bukhari, Sahih Muslim, and Sunan Abu Dawud]

Abu Sa'id ﷺ who participated in twelve ghazawat (battles) with the Prophet ﷺ said, "I heard four things from the Messenger of Allah (or I narrate them from the Prophet ﷺ) which won my admiration and appreciation. They are that: (i) no lady should travel without her husband or without a *mahram* (non-marriageable kin) for a two-day journey; (ii) no fasting is permissible on the two days of 'Id al-Fitr, and 'Id-al-Adha; (iii) no prayer (may be offered) after two prayers, after the Mid-afternoon ('Asr) prayer till the sunset, and after the Morning prayer (fajr) till the sunrises; (iv) there is no travel (for visiting) except for three Masajid, Masjid al-Haram (in Makkah), my Masjid (in Madinah), and Masjid al-Aqsa (in Jerusalem)."

[Sahih al-Bukhari]

In an era of air travel, where the world has become easily accessible, travelling to Masjid al-Aqsa should be easy. However, it is surprising to find that despite the advice of Prophet Muhammad ﷺ and the ease with which one can travel, most Muslims in the West have not visited al-Aqsa. Our selective concept of *din* has subconsciously allowed us to ignore Masjid al-Aqsa. It is important to realize that we must serve the *din* as the need requires, rather than what pleases us and is simple to carry out.

E. *Starting Hajj or 'Umrah from Masjid Al-Aqsa*

Prophet Muhammad ﷺ used all means possible to ensure that the Ummah does not forget al-Haram al-Sharif (al-Aqsa). The most sacred journey for the Muslim is the journey of Hajj or 'Umrah, and the Prophet ﷺ stated that every Muslim should consider travelling via Masjid al-Aqsa to perform these acts. It became the norm of the pious predecessors (salaf) to follow the Prophet's ﷺ advice, and they would enter their ihram (Hajj garments with the right intention) in al-Haram al-Sharif (al-Aqsa). These numerous references in the Shari'ah to al-Aqsa should ensure that it remains at the forefront of our concerns and serve as a warning to the believers against neglecting it. The advice of Prophet Muhammad ﷺ and the tradition of the pious predecessors need to be revived and believers need once again to strive to enter the state of ihram from al-Haram al-Sharif (al-Aqsa) before proceeding for Hajj or 'Umrah.

Umm Salamah ؓ, the Mother of the Faithful, relates that the Prophet ﷺ said, "If anyone puts on ihram for Hajj or 'Umrah from Masjid al-Aqsa and then proceeds to the Sacred Masjid, his former and latter sins will be forgiven, or he will be guaranteed paradise." The narrator 'Abdullah was in doubt as to which of these words ("his former and latter sins will be forgiven, or he will be guaranteed paradise") he ﷺ said.

[Sunan Abu Dawud]

"Yahya ﷺ related to me (Malik) from a reliable source that 'Abdullah ibn 'Umar once entered ihram at Iliya' (Jerusalem)."

[Imam Malik]

Some of the Companions known to have worn their ihram from al-Aqsa include, 'Umar ibn al-Khattab ﷺ, the second righteous Caliph; Sa'd ibn Abi Waqqas ﷺ; 'Abdullah ibn 'Umar ﷺ; Tamim al-Dari ﷺ; 'Amr ibn al-'As ﷺ; Abu Hurayrah ﷺ; and 'Abdullah ibn 'Abbas ﷺ.

# 6 | Al-Mi'raj

ANAS BIN MALIK ॐ narrates: "The night the Messenger of Allah ॐ was taken for a journey from the Masjid of the Ka'bah, three persons came to him (in a dream), before the Divine Inspiration was revealed to Him, while he was sleeping in the Sacred Masjid. One of them said, 'Which of them is he?' The middle (second) angel said, 'He is the best of them.' The last (third) angle said, 'Take the best of them.' Only that much happened on that night and he did not see them till they came on another night (i.e. after the Divine Inspiration was revealed to him[1]) and he saw them; his eyes were asleep but his heart was not—and so too is the case with the Prophets, their eyes sleep while their hearts do not. So those angels did not talk to him till they carried him and placed him beside the well of Zamzam. From among them Jibra'il took charge of him. Jibra'il cut open (the part of his body) between his throat and the middle of his chest (heart) and took all the material out of his chest and abdomen and then washed it with Zamzam water with his own hands, until he cleansed the inside of his body. A gold tray containing a gold bowl full of belief and wisdom was brought and then Jibra'il poured it in his chest and throat blood vessels and then closed it (the chest). He then ascended with him to the heaven and knocked on one of its doors.

"The dwellers of the heaven asked, 'Who is it?' He said, 'Jibra'il.' They said, 'Who is accompanying you?' He said, 'Muhammad.' They said, 'Has he been called?' He said, 'Yes.' They said, 'He is welcomed.' So the dwellers of the heaven became pleased with his arrival, and they did not know what

34

Allah 🕮 would do to the Prophet on earth unless Allah 🕮
informed them..."²

The Sufi al-Qushayri, in his evaluation of al-Mi'raj, draws
fascinating parallels in trying to understand the order in which
Prophet Muhammad 🕮 met the other Prophets 🕮. The seven
Prophets on the seven stations of heaven reflect, first, the meeting
with Adam 🕮 the father of the human race, who was the first of
Allah's caliphs on earth; second, the sphere of the spirit where 'Isa
🕮 is placed through whom Allah spoke to mankind; third, the
sphere of beauty where Yusuf 🕮 is seated; fourth, the sphere of
Idris through whom Allah 🕮 manifested His power; fifth, the station
of Harun 🕮 the assistance and one of command; sixth, Musa 🕮
through whom Allah sent His Law; seventh, Ibrahim 🕮 the friend
of Allah and father of all religions.³

The journey indicates that all of the Prophets, from Adam 🕮
to Muhammad 🕮 conveyed the same core message, and the journey
makes a clear indication on the transfer of the overall message to
the final Prophet, Muhammad 🕮.

## First Heaven

Anas ibn Malik narrates: "The Prophet 🕮 met Adam 🕮 over
the nearest heaven. Jibra'il said to the Prophet 🕮 'He is your
father; greet him.' The Prophet 🕮 greeted him and Adam 🕮
returned his greeting and said, 'Welcome, O my Son! O what
a good son you are!' And lo, he saw two flowing rivers, while
he was in the nearest sky. He asked, 'What are these two rivers,
O Jibra'il?' Jibra'il said, 'These are the sources of the Nile and
the Euphrates.'

"Then Jibra'il took him around that heaven and behold,
he saw another river at the bank of which there was a palace
built of pearls and emeralds. He put his hand into the river
and found its mud like musk called Adhfar. He asked, 'What
is this, O Jibra'il?' Jibra'il said, 'This is the Kawthar which
your Lord has kept for you.' Then Jibra'il ascended (with him)
to the second heaven..."⁴

## Second Heaven

"...And the angels asked the same questions as those on the first heaven. (i.e. 'Who is it?') Jibra'il replied, 'Jibrail.' They asked, 'Who is accompanying you?' He said, 'Muhammad.' They asked, 'Has he been sent for?' He said, 'Yes.' Then they said, 'He is welcome...'"[5]

"...When he 鏐 went over the second heaven... lo there was Yahya (John) and 'Isa 鏐 (Jesus) who were cousins of each other. Jibra'il said, 'These are 'Isa and Yahya; pay them your greetings.' He 鏐 said, 'I greeted them.' Both of them returned the greetings and said, 'You are welcome, O pious brother and Prophet.'"[6]

## Third Heaven

"Then he ascended until he came to the third heaven and Jibra'il asked for its gate to be opened. It was asked, 'Who is it?' Jibra'il replied, 'Jibra'il.' It was asked, 'Who is accompanying you?' Jibra'il replied, 'Muhammad.' It was asked, 'Has he been called?' 'Yes,' he replied. Then it was said, 'He is welcome; what an excellent visitor has come!' He 鏐 said, 'The gate was opened, and when I entered, there was Yusuf 鏐 (Joseph).' Jibra'il said, 'This is Yusuf; pay him your greetings.' He 鏐 said, 'So I greeted him,' and he returned the greetings, and said, 'You are welcome, O pious brother and Prophet.'"[7]

## Fourth Heaven

"Then he ascended until he came to the fourth heaven and asked for its gate to be opened. It was asked, 'Who is it?' Jibra'il replied, 'Jibra'il.' It was asked, 'Who is accompanying you?' Jibra'il replied, 'Muhammad.' It was asked, 'Has he been called?' Jibra'il replied in the affirmative. Then it was said, 'He is welcome; what an excellent visitor has come!' He 鏐 said, 'The gate was opened, and when I entered, there I saw Idris 鏐 (Enoch).' Jibra'il said, 'This is Idris; pay him your greetings.' He 鏐 said 'So I greeted him,' and he returned the greetings and said, 'You are welcome, O pious brother and Prophet.'"[8]

## Fifth Heaven

"Then he ascended until he came to the fifth heaven and asked for its gate to be opened. It was asked, 'Who is it?' Jibra'il replied, 'Jibrail.' It was asked. 'Who is accompanying you?' Jibra'il replied, 'Muhammad.' It was asked, 'Has he been called?' Jibra'il replied in the affirmative. Then it was said, 'He is welcome; what an excellent visitor has come!' He ﷺ said, 'So when I entered, there I saw Harun عليه السلام (Aaron).' Jibra'il said, 'This is Harun; pay him your greetings.' He ﷺ said, 'I greeted him,' and he returned the greetings and said, 'You are welcome, O pious brother and Prophet.'"[9]

## Sixth Heaven

"Then he ascended until he came to the sixth heaven and asked for its gate to be opened. It was asked, 'Who is it?' Jibra'il replied, 'Jibrail.' It was asked, 'Who is accompanying you?' Jibra'il replied, 'Muhammad.' It was asked, 'Has he been called?' Jibra'il replied in the affirmative. It was said, 'He is welcome; what an excellent visitor has come!' He ﷺ said, 'When I entered, there I saw Musa عليه السلام (Moses).' Jibra'il said, 'This is Musa; pay him your greeting.' He ﷺ said, 'So I greeted him,' and he returned the greetings to me and said, 'You are welcome, O pious brother and Prophet.' He ﷺ said, 'When I left him he wept.' It was said to him, 'What makes you weep?' Musa عليه السلام said, 'I weep because of a young man, who has been sent after me, and yet more people from his Community will enter Paradise than those who are from mine.'"

This hadith is quoted in Musnad Ahmed on the authority of Hadrat Anasbin Malik (Radi Allahu Anhu).

**Seventh Heaven**

"Then Jibra'il ascended with me to the seventh heaven and asked for its gate to be opened. It was asked, 'Who is it?' Jibra'il replied, 'Jibra'il.' It was asked, 'Who is accompanying you?' Jibra'il replied, 'Muhammad.' It was asked, 'Has he been called?' Jibra'il replied in the affirmative. Then it was said, 'He is welcome; what an excellent visitor has come!'So when I entered, there I saw Ibrahim ﷺ (Abraham). Jibrail said, 'This is your father; pay your greetings to him.' So I greeted him and he returned the greetings to me and said, 'You are welcome, O pious son and Prophet.'"

The Prophet ﷺ saw Ibrahim ﷺ sitting at the gate of Paradise on a throne of gold, the back of which was leaning against the Inhabited House *(bayt al-ma'mur)*. With him were a company of his people. The Prophet ﷺ greeted him and he returned his greeting and said, "Welcome to the righteous son and the righteous Prophet!"

Then Ibrahim ﷺ said, "Order your Community to increase their seedlings of Paradise for its soil is excellent and its land is plentiful." The Prophet ﷺ said, "What are the seedlings of Paradise?" He replied:

*la hawla wa la quwwata illa bi Llahi l-'ali l-'azim*
"There is no change nor might except with Allah the High, the Almighty."

Another version says, convey my greetings to your Community and tell them that Paradise has excellent soil and sweet water, and that its seedlings are:

*Subhan Allah*, Glory to Allah;
*wa l-hamdu li Llah*, and Praise to Allah;
*wa la ilaha illa Llah*, and there is no Allah but Allah;
*wa Llahu akbar*, and Allah is greatest.

**Beyond the Seventh Heaven**

The Prophet 🌸 was taken up to a point where he heard the scratching of the Pens (writing the Divine Decree). He saw a man who disappeared into the light of the Throne. He said, "Who is this? Is this an angel?" It was said to him, "No." He said, "Is it a Prophet?" Again the answer was "No". He said, "Who is it then?" The answer came, "This is a man whose tongue was moist with Allah's remembrance in the world, and his heart was attached to the Masjid, and he never incurred the curse of his father and mother."

Then the Prophet 🌸 saw his Lord, the Glorious, the Exalted, and he fell prostrate, and at that time his Lord spoke to him and said, "O Muhammad!" He replied, "At your service, O Lord!" Allah said, "Ask! (*sal*)." The Prophet 🌸 said, "You have taken to Yourself Ibrahim as a friend, and You have given him an immense kingdom. You have spoken to Musa directly, and have given Dawud an immense kingdom, and softened iron and subjected the mountains to him. You have given Sulayman an immense kingdom, and subjected the jinn and men and devils to him, as well as the winds; and You have given him a kingdom the like of which no one may have after him. You have taught 'Isa the Tawrah and the Injil, and made him heal those born blind and the lepers, and raise up the dead with Your permission; and You have protected him and his mother from the cursed Devil so that the Devil had no path by which to harm them!"

Allah 🌸 said, "And I have taken you to Myself as My beloved." The narrator said, "It is written in the Tawrah, *habibu Llah* ("Allah's Beloved"); Allah continued, "And I have sent you for all people without exception, a bearer of glad tidings and a warner; and I have expanded your breast for you and relieved you of your burden and exalted your name; and I am not mentioned except you are mentioned with Me; and I have made your Community the best Community ever brought out for the benefit of mankind; and I have made your Community a mean and a middle; and I have made your Community in truth the first and the last of all Communities;

and I have made public address (al-khutbah) impermissible for your Community unless they first witness that you are My servant and Messenger; and I have placed certain people in your Community with Evangels for hearts (i.e. repositories of Allah's Book); and I have made you the first Prophet created and the last one sent and the first one heard in My court; and I have given you Seven of the Oft-Repeated verses which I gave to no other Prophet before you (Surah al-Fatihah); and I have given you the last verses of Surah al-Baqarah which constitute a treasure from under My Throne, which I gave to no other Prophet before you; and I have given you the Kawthar; and I have given you eight arrows (shares in good fortune): Islam, emigration (hijrah), Jihad, charity (sadaqah), fasting in Ramadan, ordering good, and forbidding evil; and the day I created the heavens and the earth I made obligatory upon you and upon your Community fifty prayers, therefore establish them, you and your Community."

(Al-Shami added:) "On the authority of Abu Hurayrah ﷺ the Prophet ﷺ said, 'My Lord has preferred me over everyone else (faddalani Rabbi); He has sent me as a mercy to the worlds and to all people without exception, a bearer of glad tidings and a warner; He has thrown terror into the hearts of my enemies at a distance of a month's travel; he has made spoils of war lawful for me while they were not lawful for anyone before me; the entire earth has been made a ritually pure place of prostration for me; I was given the words that open, those that close, and those that are comprehensive in meaning (the apex of eloquence); my Community was shown to me and there is none of the followers and the followed but he is known to me; I saw that they would come to a people that wear hair-covered sandals; I saw that they would come to a people of large faces and small eyes as if they had been pierced with a needle; nothing of what they would face in the future has been kept hidden from me; and I have been ordered to perform fifty prayers daily.' And he has been given three particular merits: he is the master of the Messengers (sayyid al-mursalin), the Leader of the God-conscious (imam al-muttaqin), and the Chief of those with signs

of light on their faces and limbs (qa'id al-ghurr al-muhajjalin)."
(End of al-Shami's addition)

Then the cloud that cloaked him was dispelled and Jibra'il
took him by the hand and hurried away with him until he reached
Ibrahim ﷺ, who did not say anything.

Anas ibn Malik narrates: "Then the Prophet ﷺ reached Musa ﷺ
who asked, 'What did you do, O Muhammad? What obligations did
your Lord impose on you and your Community?' He replied, 'He
imposed fifty prayers every day and night on me and my Community.'
Musa ﷺ said, 'Return to your Lord and ask Him to lighten your
burden and that of your Community for in truth your Community
will not be able to carry it. Verily I myself have experienced people's
natures before you. I tested the Children of Israel and took the
greatest pains to hold them to something easier than this, but they
were too weak to carry it and they abandoned it. Your Community
are even weaker in their bodies and constitutions, in their hearts, in
their sight, and in their hearing.'

"The Prophet ﷺ turned to Jibra'il to consult him. The
latter indicated to him that yes, if you wish, then return. The
Prophet ﷺ hurried back until he reached the Tree and the
cloud cloaked him and he fell prostrate. Then he said, 'Lord,
make lighter the burden of my Community for verily they are
the weakest of all Communities.' He replied, 'I have removed
five prayers from their obligation.'

"Then the cloud was dispelled and the Prophet ﷺ returned
to Musa ﷺ and told him, 'He has removed five prayers from
my obligation.' He replied, 'Go back to your Lord and ask
him to make it less, for in truth your Community will not be
able to carry that.' The Prophet ﷺ did not cease to go back
and forth between Musa ﷺ and his Lord, while Allah ﷻ
each time reduced it by five prayers, until Allah ﷻ said, 'O
Muhammad!' The Prophet ﷺ said, 'At Your service, O Lord!'
He said, 'Let them be five prayers every day and night, and let
every prayer count as ten. That makes fifty prayers. This word

of Mine shall not be changed nor shall My Book be abrogated. Let whoever is about to perform a good deed, even if he does not ultimately do it, receive the reward of doing it, while if he does it, he shall receive it tenfold. Let whoever is about to commit a bad deed, and he does not ultimately do it, let not anything be written against him, while if he does it, let one misdeed be written against him.'

"Then the cloud was dispelled and the Prophet ﷺ returned to Musa ﷺ and told him, 'He has removed [another] five prayers from my obligation.' He replied, 'Go back to your Lord and ask him to make it less, for in truth your Community will not be able to carry that.' The Prophet ﷺ said, 'I have gone back again and again to my Lord and now I feel shy. Rather, I accept and submit.'(At this a herald called out, 'I have decreed My obligation and have reduced the burden of My servants.') Musa ﷺ then said to the Prophet ﷺ, 'Go down in the name of Allah.'"[10]

# 7 | Experiences and Eyewitness Account

WHILE ON THE journey of al-Mi'raj, the Prophet 🕮 witnessed specific events which helped portray an image of the hereafter as a life based on the consequences for deeds committed on earth. His 🕮 glimpses of heaven and hell should help a believer consolidate the message of the Holy Qur'an regarding the life to come. Hence, al-Isra' and al-Mi'raj helps re-affirm to a believer the faith and humbles him to the power of the Almighty.

### Swimming in Three Different Rivers
When Prophet Muhammad 🕮 met with Ibrahim 🕮, he saw him sitting in the company of two types of people; one group had pure white faces and next to them were people with blemishes on their faces. The latter group stood and entered a river in which they bathed. They then came out having purified some of their blemishes. They then entered another river and bathed and came out, having further purified their blemishes. They then entered a third river and bathed and purified themselves and their hue became like that of the first group. Thereafter they came and joined the company of the first group.

The Prophet 🕮 said, "O Jibra'il, who are those with white faces and those who had blemishes on their faces, and what are these rivers in which they entered and bathed?" Jibra'il replied, "The ones with white faces are a people who never tarnished their belief with injustice or disobedience; those with blemishes on their faces are a people who would mix good deeds with bad ones, then they repented and Allah ﷻ relented towards them. As for these rivers; the first is Allah's mercy (*rahmatu Llah*); the second is His favour (*ni'matu Llah*); and the third, a pure drink - 'and their Lord gave them a pure beverage to drink (*wa saqahum Rabbuhum sharaban tahuran*)'." (76:21)

### Prophet's Community

The Prophet ﷺ witnessed two communities. He was told, "This is your place and the place of your Community." He saw that his Community was divided into two halves; one half wearing clothes that were pure and white, the other wearing dark and dusty clothes. He entered the Oft-frequented House (Bayt al-ma'mur), and those who were wearing the white clothes entered with him. Those who wore ash-coloured clothes were no longer able to see him, and yet they were in the best of states. The Prophet ﷺ prayed in the House together with those of the believers who were with him.

One version states that the presentation of the three drinks to the Prophet ﷺ and his choice of milk, and Jibra'il's approval, took place at this point.

### Lote Tree

The Prophet ﷺ said: "I was raised up to the Lote-tree of the Farthest Boundary (there ends whatever ascends from the earth before it is seized, and whatever descends from above before it is seized). And lo, its fruits were like the jars of Hijr (a place near Madinah) and its leaves were as big as the ears of elephants. Jibra'il said, 'This is the Lote-tree of the Farthest Boundary.' And lo, there ran four rivers; two were hidden and two were visible. I asked, 'What are these two kinds of rivers, O Jibra'il?' He replied, 'As for the hidden rivers, they are two rivers in Paradise and the visible rivers are the Nile and the Euphrates.'"[1]

Al-Dardir ﷺ said, "This is the eighth ascension, meaning that it is the ascension to what is higher than the Lote-tree by means of the eighth step, so that the Prophet ﷺ reached the top height of its branches in the eighth firmament, which is called *al-Kursi* - the Chair, or Footstool - which is made of a white pearl."

The general consensus is that the base of the Lote-tree is on the sixth heaven, while its top branches traverse to the seventh heaven. "Then he was raised to the Lote-tree of the Farthest Boundary" indicates that the eighth ascension took place at that later point and that the present stage is only an exposition of his coming to the base of the Tree, which is in the seventh heaven. Another narration states that it is in the sixth heaven. What harmonizes the two is that its base is in the sixth heaven while its branches and trunk are in the seventh.

It is a tree from the base of which issue rivers whose water are never brackish (it does not change in taste, or colour, or smell, and the sweat of those who drink it in Paradise has the fragrance of musk); and rivers of milk whose taste does not change after it is drunk; and rivers of wine which bring only pleasure to those who drink it; and rivers of purified honey. Someone on his mount could travel under the tree's shade for seventy years and still not come out of it. The lotus fruit that grows on it resembles the jars of Hijr (near Madinah). Its leaves are shaped like the ears of the she-elephant, and each leaf could wrap up this Community entirely. One version says that one of its leaves could wrap up all creatures.

On top of each leaf there was an angel who covered it with colours which cannot be described. Whenever he covered it, by Allah's order it would change. One version says that it would turn into sapphire and chrysolite, the beauty of which is impossible for anyone to praise or compare. On it were moths of gold.

Ibn Kathir (Allah have mercy on him) states, "What is meant by this, and Allah ﷻ knows best, is that these two rivers (the Nile and the Euphrates) resemble the rivers of Paradise in their purity and sweetness and fluidity and such of their qualities, as the Prophet ﷺ said in the hadith narrated by Abu Hurayrah ؓ, 'Date pastry is from Paradise' (*al-'ajwah min al-jannah*); that is, it resembles the fruit of Paradise, not that it itself originates in Paradise. For if that were the meaning then the senses would testify to the contrary. Therefore the meaning which imposes itself is other than that. Similarly, the source of origin of these rivers is on earth."

(Al-Shami added) "One version says, 'At the base of the tree ran a source called Salsabil. From it issued two rivers, one is the Kawthar.' (The Prophet ﷺ said,) 'I saw it flowing impetuously, roaring, at the speed of arrows. Near it were pavilions of pearl (lu'lu'), sapphire (yaqut), and chrysolite (zabarjad), on top of which nested green birds more delicate than any you have ever seen. On its banks were vessels of gold and silver. It ran over pebbles made of sapphire and emerald (zumurrud). Its water was whiter than milk.'

"The Prophet ﷺ took one of the vessels and scooped some water and drank. It was sweeter than honey and more fragrant than musk. Jibra'il said to him, 'This is the river which Allah has given you as a special gift, and the other river is the River of Mercy.' The Prophet ﷺ bathed in it and his past and future sins were forgiven." (End of al-Shami's addition)

One version says: "At the Lote-tree of the Farthest Boundary the Prophet ﷺ saw Jibra'il (in his angelic form). He had six hundred wings. Every single wing could cover the entire firmament. From his wings embellishments were strewn in all directions, such as rare pearls and sapphires of a kind Allah ﷻ alone knows." Then the Prophet ﷺ was taken to the Kawthar and entered Paradise. Lo and behold! It contains what no eye has seen, nor ear heard, nor human mind ever imagined. Allah's Apostle ﷺ said: "On the night I was made to ascend (the heavens), I saw written on the gate of paradise: (al-sadaqat bi 'ashr amthaliha; wa al-qard bi thamaniyat 'asharah) 'Charity is repaid tenfold; and loan eighteenfold.' The Prophet ﷺ said, 'O Jibra'il, how can the loan be more meritorious than charity?' He replied, 'Because the one asking for charity may still have something, while the borrower does not borrow except out of need.'"

The Prophet ﷺ continued to travel until he reached rivers of milk whose taste does not change, and rivers of wine which bring only pleasure to those who drink it, and rivers of honey purified, and overhanging those rivers were domes of hollowed pearl whose circumference is like the Aquarius star.

Another narration says, "Above the rivers were pommels resembling the hides of the humped camels. Its birds were like the Bactrian camel. Upon hearing this Abu Bakr ﷺ said, 'O Messenger of Allah, they are certainly delicate!' The Prophet ﷺ replied, 'And daintier to eat yet, and certainly I hope that you shall eat from them.'"

(This is an indication of the rank of Abu Bakr ﷺ in Paradise, as the Prophet's hope, like his petition, is granted. Sheikh Muhammad ibn 'Alawi said, 'From all this it can be known that Paradise and the Fire exist already, that the Lote-tree of the Farthest Boundary is outside Paradise.)

Then the Fire was shown to him. In it he saw Allah's wrath and His punishment and sanction. Where rocks and iron to be thrown into it, the Fire would consume them completely. In it were a people who were eating carrion. The Prophet ﷺ said: "Who are these, O Jibra'il?" He replied, "Those who ate the flesh of people."

Then the Prophet ﷺ saw Malik, the custodian of the Fire. He was a grim figure whose face expressed anger. The Prophet ﷺ greeted him first.[2] Then the gates of the Fire were closed as he stood outside, and he was raised up beyond the Lote-tree of the Farthest Boundary, and a cloud concealed him from everything else, and Jibra'il stayed back.

**The Farthest Limit—Meeting Allah ﷻ**

There is a difference of opinion as to whether the Prophet ﷺ saw Allah ﷻ, and if he did, whether it was with his "earthly" eyes. The majority of the Companions took the view from the authority of Ibn 'Abbas ﷺ, who was of the opinion that the Prophet ﷺ saw Allah ﷻ with his physical eyes.

However, 'A'ishah ﷺ, on the other hand, does not agree. Al-Bukhari quotes Masruq ﷺ that he asked 'A'ishah ﷺ:

"O Mother, did the Prophet ﷺ see his Lord?" She said, "What you ask me makes my hair stand on end. I shall tell you three things, which if anyone says they are true, they are lying." Then she recited: *"No power of vision can encompass Him, whereas He encompasses all vision; He is above all comprehension, yet is All-aware (al-Anam 6:103)*; and *"It is not fitting for a man that Allah should speak to him except by inspiration or from behind a veil (al-Shura 42:51)*. Then she went on to say, "Whoever tells you that the Prophet 🕌 knows what will happen tomorrow is a liar. Whoever tells you that he concealed anything is a liar. But he 🕌 saw Jibra'il in his true form twice."

She maintained that the verses in Surah al-Najm: "And he approached and came closer" and "For indeed he saw him at a second descent. By the Sidrat al-Muntaha" (53:8–14) refers to the Prophet 🕌 seeing Jibra'il.

إِنْ هُوَ إِلَّا وَحْىٌ يُوحَىٰ ۞ عَلَّمَهُ شَدِيدُ ٱلْقُوَىٰ ۞ ذُو مِرَّةٍ فَٱسْتَوَىٰ ۞ وَهُوَ بِٱلْأُفُقِ ٱلْأَعْلَىٰ ۞ ثُمَّ دَنَا فَتَدَلَّىٰ ۞ فَكَانَ قَابَ قَوْسَيْنِ أَوْ أَدْنَىٰ ۞ فَأَوْحَىٰ إِلَىٰ عَبْدِهِۦ مَا أَوْحَىٰ ۞ مَا كَذَبَ ٱلْفُؤَادُ مَا رَأَىٰ ۞ أَفَتُمَـٰرُونَهُۥ عَلَىٰ مَا يَرَىٰ ۞ وَلَقَدْ رَءَاهُ نَزْلَةً أُخْرَىٰ ۞ عِندَ سِدْرَةِ ٱلْمُنتَهَىٰ ۞

*"That [which he delivers to you] is nothing less than a revelation sent down to him. Something that a very mighty one has taught him, of surpassing power, who stood on the highest horizon, and then drew near, and came close, until he was two bow-lengths away, or even closer, and revealed to Allah's servant what he revealed. (Muhammad's) heart did not believe what he saw. Will you then contend with him over what he sees? Indeed he saw a second time by the Lote-tree of the Farthest Boundary..."*

(Al-Najm 53:4–14)

According to 'A'ishah 🌸 the "very mighty one" is Jibra'il. The Prophet 🕌 saw him in his original form and size as Allah 🕌 created him, covering the horizon with his enormous body, with his six hundred wings unfurled. He then drew near and came closer towards the Prophet 🕌 until he was very near to him or as the Surah says, "Two bows-length, or even closer".

However, Ibn 'Abbas ⬥ used to prove and firmly believed that the Prophet ⬥ did actually see Allah ⬥ on that night. The majority of the scholars ('ulama') have supported this view.

Imam al-Nawawi (Allah have mercy on him) writes, "The crux of this issue is the hadith of Ibn 'Abbas. Once, Ibn 'Umar ⬥ asked him, 'Did Prophet Muhammad ⬥ see his Lord?' He replied, 'Yes.'

"The hadith of 'A'ishah ⬥ does not contradict the view of Ibn 'Abbas ⬥ since her interpretation is from the Holy Qur'an rather than the statement of the Prophet ⬥. 'A'ishah ⬥ does not state that she heard the Prophet ⬥ say, 'I did not see my Lord.' Instead, whatever she said was her interpretation of the Qur'anic verses 'It is not fitting for a human that Allah should speak to him except by inspiration...' (42:51) and 'no vision can grasp Him, but His grasp is over all vision...' (6.103)

"However, since the narrations of Ibn 'Abbas ⬥, which confirm the Prophet's ⬥ having seen Allah ⬥, are on a strong chain of narrators, it becomes necessary to accept that the Prophet ⬥ did see Allah ⬥. Furthermore, one cannot possibly imagine the declaration of Ibn 'Abbas on such an issue to be based on his own personal opinion and judgment" (al-Nawawi on *Sahih Muslim*).

The Holy Qur'an informs us in Surah al-Qiyamah that people in the hereafter will see their Lord:

$$وُجُوهٌ يَوْمَئِذٍ نَّاضِرَةٌ ۝ إِلَىٰ رَبِّهَا نَاظِرَةٌ ۝$$

*Some faces that Day, will beam (in brightness and beauty) - looking towards their Lord...*

(Al-Qiyamah 75:22–3)

Since it is evidently clear that humans will be able to see their Lord due to Allah's ⬥ leave, we can deduce it was made possible for the Prophet ⬥ to see his Lord. Imam Malik said, "Man cannot see Allah in this life, since Allah is eternal and man is finite and the finite cannot grasp the eternal. But in the hereafter when the believers will have been given their eternal (life) and vision, the Eternal (Lord) will be seen."

Abu Amamah ﷺ reports that he heard the Prophet ﷺ say, "Know that none of you will see your Lord until you die."[3]

### Encounter with the Devil

As the Prophet ﷺ was travelling mounted on the Buraq he saw a devil from the jinn, who was trying to get near him holding a flame of fire. Everywhere the Prophet ﷺ turned he would see him. Jibra'il said to him, "Shall I teach you words which, if you say them, his fire will be extinguished and cause it to fall?" The Prophet ﷺ said, "Yes." Jibra'il said:

> "Say:[4] (*A'udhu bi wajhi Llahi l-Karim; wa bi kalimati Llahi t-tammati l-lati la yujawizuhunna barrun wa la fajir; min sharri ma yanzilu min s-sama'; wa min sharri ma ya'ruju fiha; wa min sharri ma dhara'a fi l-ard; wa min sharri ma yakhruju minha; wa min fitani l-layli wa n-nahar; wa min tawariq l-layli wa n-nahar; illa tariqin yatruqu bi khayrin ya Rahman*).
>
> I seek refuge in the Face of Allah the Munificent; and in Allah's perfect words, which neither the righteous nor the disobedient overstep; from the evil of what descends from the heaven and the evil of what ascends to it; and the evil of what is created in the earth; and the trials of the night and the day; and the visitors of the night and the day; except the visitor that comes with goodness; O Beneficent One!"

At this the devil fell dead on his face and his firebrand went out.

### Performing Salah en route and meeting Musa ﷺ

While travelling on the Buraq they reached a land filled with date-palms. Jibra'il said to the Prophet ﷺ, "Alight and pray here." He did so and remounted, and then Jibra'il said, "Do you know where you prayed?" He said, "No." Jibra'il said, "You prayed in a *taybah* (land of pastures) and the emigration will take place there."

They continued their journey on the Buraq and after a while Jibra'il again said, "Alight and pray here." He did so and remounted, and then Jibra'il said, "Do you know where you prayed?" He said, "No." Jibra'il said, "You prayed in Madyan (a city on the shore of the Red Sea, bordering Tabuk near the valley of Shu'ayb) at the tree of Musa (where Musa rested from fatigue and hunger during his flight from Fir'awn [Pharaoh])." They continued their journey, and then Jibra'il said again, "Alight and pray here." He did so and remounted, and then Jibrail said, "Do you know where you prayed?" He said, "No." Jibra'il said, "You prayed at Mount Sinai, where Allah ﷻ addressed Musa." Then he reached a land where the palaces of Syria became visible to him. Jibra'il said to him, "Alight and pray." He did so and remounted, and then the Buraq continued his lightning flight and Jibra'il said, "Do you know where you prayed?" He said, "No." Jibra'il said, "You prayed in Bayt Lahm (Bethlehem), where 'Isa ibn Maryam was born."

> Anas ibn Malik ؓ reports the Messenger ﷺ saying, "On the night in which I was taken on the journey, I passed by Musa near the red hill and found him saying his prayers in his grave."
>
> [Sahih Muslim]

In a hadith qudsi the Prophet ﷺ narrates the incident of how the soul of Musa ﷺ was taken. Abu Hurayrah ؓ reports that the Prophet ﷺ said, "The angel of death was sent to Musa. When he came to Musa, Musa slapped him on the eye. The angel returned to Allah ﷻ and said, 'You have sent me to a servant who does not want to die.' Allah ﷻ ordered the angel, 'Return to him and tell him to put his hand on the back of an ox and for every hair that will come under it, he will be granted one year of life.' Musa said, 'O Lord! What will happen after that?' Allah ﷻ replied, 'Then death.' Musa decided, 'Let it be now.' Musa then requested Allah ﷻ to let him die close to the Sacred Land, so much so that he would be at a distance of a stone's throw from it." Abu Hurayrah ؓ added that the Prophet ﷺ then said, "If I were there, I would show you his grave below the red sand hill on the side of the road."

[Sahih al-Bukhari]

### Lips slashed with shears

Anas ⚖ reports that the Prophet ﷺ said, "On the night of al-Mi'raj, I saw some people whose lips were being slit with scissors of fire. I asked Jibra'il who these people were and he replied that they are the sermonizers (khutaba') who commanded people to do good deeds while not practising what they preached." In another version of this hadith it says, "They are the sermonizers (of your Ummah) who say such things which they themselves do not do. They read the Book of Allah ﷻ, without themselves practising upon it."[5]

### Chest Scraped with Fingernails

Anas ⚖ reports that the Prophet ﷺ said, "When I was taken up during the night of al-Mi'raj, I passed by people who had fingernails of copper and they were raking their own faces and chests with them. I asked Jibra'il who they were and he replied that they were those who used to eat the flesh of others (i.e. slandered them) and attacked their reputations."[6]

### Swimming in Blood

The Prophet ﷺ saw a man swimming in a river of blood and he was being struck in his mouth with rocks, which he then swallowed. The Prophet ﷺ asked, "What is this, O Jibra'il?" He replied, "This is what happens to those who eat usury."

### Stomachs the Size of Houses

Another form of severe punishment for engaging in transactions of usury is indicated by a hadith on the authority of Abu Hurayrah ⚖ who reports that the Prophet ﷺ said: "On the night of al-Mi'raj I passed by people whose bellies were as huge as houses; and inside their bellies were snakes which were visible from the outside. I asked Jibra'il who they were. He replied that they were those who consume interest (usury)."[7]

## The Importance of Cupping

'Abdullah ibn Mas'ud ☼ narrates, "Among the things described by the Prophet ☼ about the Night Journey was that every group of angels he passed by, urged him to instruct his Ummah to practise cupping."[8]

## Instantaneous Harvesting of Seeds

They travelled until they reached a people who sowed seeds and within a day reaped the harvest. Every time they reaped, their harvest would be replenished as before. The Prophet ☼ said, "O Jibra'il, what is this?" He replied, "These are the *mu-jahidun* - those who strive in the path of Allah ☼ the Exalted. Every good deed of theirs is multiplied for them seven hundred times, and whatever they spend returns multiplied."

## Fir'awn's Servant

The Prophet ☼ then experienced a fragrant wind and asked, "O Jibra'il, what is this sweet scent?" He replied, "This is the scent of the lady who combed the hair of Fir'awn's daughter and that of her children. As she combed the hair of Fir'awn's daughter the comb fell and she said, *bismiLlah* ('In the name of Allah'), whereupon Fir'awn's daughter said, 'Do you have a Lord other than my father?' She said, 'Yes.' Fir'awn's daughter said, 'Shall I tell my father?' She said, 'Fine.' She told Fir'awn and he summoned her and questioned her, 'Do you have a Lord other than me?' She replied, 'Yes, my Lord and your Lord is Allah.'

"Fir'awn summoned her two sons and husband and he began to entice the woman and her husband to renege on their religion, but they refused. Upon their resistance he warned that unless they renege upon believing in Allah ☼ he would kill them. She said, 'Be so good as to bury us all together in a single grave if you kill us.' He replied, 'Granted, and it is your right to ask us.' He then ordered that a huge structure of copper in the image of a cow be made. He filled this with boiling liquid and commanded his soldiers to throw the woman and her children into the cauldron. The children were taken and thrown in one after the other. The second and youngest was still an infant at the breast. When they took him he said, 'Mother! Jump and do not tarry for verily you are on the right.' Then she was thrown in with her children."

Ibn 'Abbas ﷺ said, "Four spoke from the cradle as they were still infants: 'Isa ibn Maryam (upon whom be peace), Jurayj's companion, Yusuf's witness (12:26), and the son of Mashitah (the servant who combed the hair of Fir'awn's daughter)."[9]

### Heads Crushed with Rocks

The Prophet ﷺ reported that they passed by a group of people whose heads were being crushed with boulders. After being smashed, their heads would resume their original shape, only to be crushed again. This process continued ceaselessly. When he asked Jibra'il who they were, he replied that these were the people who were neglectful of their salah. In another narration it states, "These are the people whose heads were too heavy (on their pillows) to get up and fulfil the prescribed prayers."

### Grazing Like Animals

The Prophet ﷺ reported that they passed by a group of people whose private parts, from the front and behind, were wrapped in rags and they were grazing like camels and cattle. They were eating *Dari*, a thorny plant (from Jahannam), *Zaqqum* (a most bitter and foul smelling tree, growing at the bottom of Jahannam) and the smouldering stones of Jahannam. The Prophet ﷺ asked Jibra'il who these people were. He replied, "They are those who do not discharge the zakah of their wealth."

**Eating Foul Meat**

The Prophet ﷺ then passed by a group of people in front of whom were two types of meat. In one plate was some cooked meat and in the other plate was foul decaying meat. Despite the good cooked meat he saw these people eating the decaying meat. The Prophet ﷺ asked Jibra'il who they were, and he replied, "These are the men from your Community who had an excellent, lawful wife at home and who would go and see a foul woman and spend the night with her; and the women who would leave their excellent, lawful husbands to go and see foul men and spend the night with them."

**Burdened With Carrying Wood**

Then he saw a man who had gathered a stack of wood, which he could not carry, yet he was adding more wood to it. He said, "What is this, O Jibra'il?" He replied, "This is a man from your Community who gets people's trusts when he cannot fulfil them, yet he insists on carrying them."

**Crossing a Razor-Sharp Road**

Then he came to a plank in the middle of the road, which not even a piece of cloth nor less than that could cross except it would be pierced. He said, "What is this, O Jibra'il?" He replied, "This is what happens to those of your Community who sit in the middle of the road and cut it," and he recited,

وَلَا تَقْعُدُواْ بِكُلِّ صِرَاطٍ تُوعِدُونَ وَتَصُدُّونَ عَن سَبِيلِ ٱللَّهِ مَنْ ءَامَنَ بِهِۦ
وَتَبْغُونَهَا عِوَجًا ... ﴾

*Lurk not on every road to threaten wayfarers and to turn away from Allah's path he who believes in Him, and to seek to make it crooked*
(Al-'Araf 7:86)

This verse refers to some of the people of Shu'ayb who were involved in corruption, threatening people and preventing them from attending to their business. They were also wrongdoers, trying to turn those who believe away from their faith, making it difficult for them to follow the right path and trying to show Allah's straight path as crooked.

### An Ox Attempts to Enter a Pin Hole

The Prophet ﷺ thereafter witnessed a huge ox emerge from a tiny hole. The ox thereafter tried to re-enter the hole. The Prophet ﷺ asked who this was and Jibra'il replied that this was the person who, after having uttered some very serious and sinful words, was full of remorse and wished to retract them but was unable to do so.

### The Fragrance of Jannah

The Prophet ﷺ reached a valley from which a very beautiful fragrance emanated. The smell was of musk and it possessed a voice. The Prophet ﷺ asked, "What is this?" Jibra'il replied that it is the voice of Jannah saying, "O My Lord! Bring to me those people who have been destined to stay in me, and fulfil your promise."

(Al-Shami added:) "He then came to a valley in which he breathed a sweet, cool breeze fragrant with musk and he heard a voice. He said, 'What is this, O Jibra'il?' He replied, 'This is the voice of Paradise saying, "O my Lord, bring me what You have promised me for too abundant are my rooms, my gold-laced garments, my silk, my brocades, my carpets, my pearls, my coral, my silver, my gold, my goblets, my bowls, my pitchers, my couches, my honey, my water, my milk, my wine!" And He ﷻ says, "You will have every Muslim man and woman, every believing man and woman, and everyone who has believed in Me and My Messengers and did excellent deeds without associating a partner to Me nor taking helpers without Me. Anyone who fears Me will be safe, and whoever asks Me I shall give him, and whoever lends Me something I shall repay him, and whoever relies on Me I shall suffice him. I am Allah besides whom there is no god. I never fail in My promise. Successful indeed are the believers! Blessed is Allah, therefore, the Best of Creators!" And Paradise answered, "I accept"."

## The Foulness of Jahannam

Then he ﷺ came to a valley in which he heard a distressing sound and smelled a stench-carrying wind. He said, "What is this, O Jibra'il?" He replied, "This is the sound of Jahannam saying, 'O Lord, give me what You promised me, for abundant are my chains, my yokes, my punishments, my fires, my thistles, my pus, my tortures! My depth is abysmal, my heat is extreme; therefore give me what You promised me!' And He ﷻ replied, 'You will have every idolater and idolatress, every male and female disbeliever and every foul one and every tyrant who does not believe in the Day of Reckoning'."

## Greetings

As the Prophet ﷺ was travelling he heard someone calling him from his right, "O Muhammad, look at me, I want to ask you something!" But the Prophet ﷺ did not respond. Then he said, "Who was that, O Jibra'il?" He replied, "That was the herald of the Jews. If you had answered him, your Community would have followed Judaism."

The Prophet ﷺ continued travelling and he heard someone calling him from his left, "O Muhammad, look at me, I want to ask you something!" But the Prophet ﷺ did not respond. Then he said, "Who was that, O Jibra'il?" He replied, "That was the herald of the Christians. If you had answered him, your Community would have followed Christianity."

The Prophet ﷺ continued travelling and then passed by a woman with bare arms, decked with every female ornament Allah ﷻ has created. She said, "O Muhammad, look at me, I need to ask you something." But he did not look at her. Then he said, "Who was that, O Jibra'il?" He replied, "That was the world (al-dunya). If you had answered her, your Community would have preferred the world to the hereafter."

As the Prophet ﷺ travelled on, he passed by an old man who was a distance away from his path saying, "Come hither, O Muhammad!" But Jibra'il said, "Nay; go on, O Muhammad!" The Prophet ﷺ went on and then said, "Who was that, O Jibra'il?" He replied, "That was Allah's enemy, Iblis. He wanted you to incline towards him."

He went on and passed by an old woman on the roadside who said, "O Muhammad, look at me, I need to ask you something." But he did not look at her. Then he said, "Who was that, O Jibra'il?" He replied, "The world has as much time left to live as the remaining lifetime of this old woman."

## Al-Sham

The Prophet ﷺ saw a pearl-like white column, which the angels were carrying. He said, "What is this you are carrying?" They replied, "The Column of Islam. We have been ordered to place it in al-Sham (modern day Lebanon, Syria, Jordan and Palestine)."

The Prophet ﷺ called al-Sham the purest of Allah's lands, the place where religion, belief and safety are found in the time of dissension, and the home of the saints for whose sake Allah ﷻ sends sustenance to the people and victory to Muslims over their enemies:

1.  Ibn 'Asakir in *Tahdhib ta'rikh Dimashq al-kabir* relates from Ibn Mas'ud ؓ that the Prophet ﷺ compared the world to a little rain water on a mountain plateau of which the *safw* or purity had already been drunk and from which only the *kadar* or dregs remained. Al-Huwjiri and al-Qushayri mention it in their chapters on tasawwuf, respectively in *Kashf al-mahjub* and *al-Risalah al-Qushayriyyah*. Ibn al-Kathir defines *safw* and *safwa* in his dictionary *al-Nihaya* as "the best of any matter, its quintessence, and purest part". The quintessence spoken of by the Prophet ﷺ is al-Sham, because he called al-Sham "the quintessence of Allah's lands" (*safwat Allah min biladih*). Al-Tabarani related it from 'Irbad ibn Sariya and Haythami authenticated the chain of transmission in his book *Majma' al-zawa'id*, under the chapter entitled *Bab fada'il al-Sham* (the virtues of the Levant).

2.  Abu al-Darda' ؓ narrated that the Prophet ﷺ said, "As I was sleeping I saw the Column of the Book being carried away

from under my head. I feared lest it would be taken away, so I followed it with my eyes and saw that it was being planted in al-Sham. Verily, belief in the time of dissensions will be in al-Sham."

Al-Haythami said that Ahmad narrated it with a chain whose narrators are all the men of the *sahih* - sound narrations - and that al-Bazzar narrated it with a chain whose narrators are the men of sound ahadith except for Muhammad ibn 'Amir al-Antaki, and he is trustworthy (*thiqah*).

In the version al-Tabarani narrated from Ibn 'Amr in *al-Mu'jam al-kabir* and *al-Mu'jam al-awsat* the Prophet ﷺ repeats three times, "When the dissensions take place, belief will be in al-Sham." One manuscript says, "Safety will be in al-Sham." Al-Haythami said that the men in its chain are those of sound ahadith except for Ibn Lahi'a, and he is fair (*hasan*).

3.  Al-Tabarani relates from 'Abdullah ibn Hawwala ؓ that the Prophet ﷺ said, "I saw on the night that I was enraptured a white column resembling a pearl, which the angels were carrying. I said to them, 'What are you carrying?' They replied, 'The Column of the Book. We have been ordered to place it in al-Sham.' Later, in my sleep, I saw that the Column of the Book was snatched away from under my headrest (*wisadati*). I began to fear lest Allah the Almighty had abandoned the people of the earth. My eyes followed where it went. It was a brilliant light in front of me. Then I saw it was placed in al-Sham."

4.  Zayd ibn Thābit ؓ reports that the Prophet ﷺ said, "How blessed is al-Shām! The Companions around asked, "Why is that?" The Messenger ﷺ replied, "I see the angels of Allah ﷻ spread their wings over al-Shām." Ibn 'Abbās ؓ added, "And the Prophets lived in it. There is not a single inch in al-Quds (Jerusalem) where a Prophet has not prayed or an angel not stood." [Tirmidhī and Imām Aḥmad]

5. Prophet Muḥammad ﷺ is reported to have said, "Allah ﷻ has blessed what lies between al-Arish (in Egypt) and the Euphrates and has made Palestine particularly holy." [Kanz al-'Umāl]

6. Maymūnah bint Sa'd ؓ reports that she asked the Prophet ﷺ, "O Messenger of Allah, give us a pronouncement about al-Quds (Jerusalem)." The Prophet ﷺ replied, "It is the land where they will be raised (al-Ḥashr) and gathered (al-Maḥshar)." [Imām Ahamd and al-Ṭabarānī]

7. 'Awf ibn Mālik ؓ reports that the Prophet ﷺ said, "The world will be destroyed forty years before al-Shām is." [Ibn 'Asākir]

8. The Messenger of Allah ﷺ said regarding the inhabitants of the blessed land, "They and their wives, children, and slaves (men and women) are in *ribāṭ* ('guardians', literally a fort) in the cause of Allah ﷻ." [Al-Ṭabarānī]

9. Umāmah al-Bahilī ؓ reports that the Prophet ﷺ said, "A group of my Community will remain on truth, they will vanquish their enemy, and those who disagree with them will not be able to harm them until Allah ﷻ commands." "Where are these people?" The Companions asked. The Prophet ﷺ replied, "In and around al-Quds (Jerusalem)." [Imām Aḥmad]

10. Mu'āwiyah ibn Abū Sufyān ؓ relates that the Prophet ﷺ said, "There is a group among my followers who will continue to be openly on the truth. No one who opposes them will harm them until the coming of the Hour." The Companions asked, "Where will they be?" The Messenger ﷺ replied, "They will be in and around Bayt al-Maqdis." [Imām Aḥmad]

11. Abū Hurayrah ؓ relates that the Prophet ﷺ said, "A group of my Community will not cease to fight at the gates of Damascus and at the gates of al-Quds (Jerusalem) and its surroundings. The betrayal or desertion of whoever deserts

them will not harm them in the least. They will remain victorious, standing for truth, until the Final Hour rises." [Al-Ṭabarānī]

12. 'Abdullāh ibn 'Umar ﷺ reports that the Prophet ﷺ said, "There will be migration upon migration. The best of the inhabitants of the earth will reside where Prophet Ibrāhīm ﷺ migrated (Jerusalem)." [Sunan Abū Dāwūd]

13. Once the Prophet ﷺ advised 'Abdullāh ibn Hawwāla ﷺ to join the army in al-Shām, over any other. However, the Prophet ﷺ noticing Ibn Hawwāla's indifference said, "Do you know what Allah ﷻ says about al-Shām? Allah ﷻ has said, 'Al-Sham you are the quintessence of My lands (safwatī min bilādī) and I shall inhabit you with the chosen ones among My servants.'" [Al-Tabarānī]

14. 'Abdullāh ibn 'Amr ﷺ reports that the Prophet ﷺ repeated the following statement three times, "When the dissension take place belief shall be in al-Shām." One version of ḥadīth states, "Safety will be in al-Shām." [Al-Ṭabarānī]

15. 'Abdullāh ibn Hawwāla reports that the Prophet ﷺ said, "At some point you will be (split into) standing armies, one army in al-Shām, one in Yemen and one in Iraq." 'Abdullāh ibn Hawwāla asked the Prophet ﷺ, "Choose for me, Messenger of Allah, in case I live to see that day." The Prophet ﷺ replied, "You must go to al-Shām, for it is the chosen land of Allah in all His earth. He protects, by sending them there, the chosen ones among His servants. If you do not wish to go there, then go to Yemen. Allah ﷻ has given me a guarantee concerning al-Shām and its people." (Abū Idrīs al-Khawlānī would add after narrating the above hadith, "And whoever has Allah as his guarantor shall never suffer loss.") [Sunan Abū Dāwūd and Imam Aḥmad]

16. Imam Ahmad ibn Hanbal relates in his *Musnad* (1,112), The people of Syria were mentioned in front of 'Ali ibn Abi Talib

while he was in Iraq, and they said to him, "Curse them, O Commander of the Believers." He replied, "No, I heard the Messenger of Allah ﷺ say, 'The Substitutes (al-abdal) are in Syria and they are forty men, every time one of them dies, Allah ﷻ substitutes another in his place. By means of them Allah ﷻ brings down the rain, gives (Muslims) victory over their enemies and averts punishment from the people of Syria.'"

### Meassage and Greetings from Ibrahim ﷺ

'Abdullah ibn Mas'ud ؓ reports that the Prophet ﷺ said, "On the night of my Ascent (al-Mi'raj), I met Prophet Ibrahim ﷺ and he said to me, 'O Muhammad! Convey my salam to your Ummah and inform them that Paradise is a vast plain of pure soil and sweet water and that its trees recite, "Holy is Allah, all praise is due to Allah, there is none worthy of worship but Allah and Allah is Great (Subhana Llahi wa l-hamdu li Llahi wa la ilaha illa Llahu wa Llahu akbar)." [Al-Tirmidhi]

### Loan Better Than Charity

As mentioned earlier (under the Lote-tree), when the Prophet ﷺ entered Paradise he saw what no eye has seen, nor ear heard, nor human mind ever imagined. On its gate he saw written:

*al-sadaqah bi 'ashrin amthaliha, wa al-qard bi thamaniyati 'asharah*
Charity is repaid tenfold, and loan eighteenfold.

The Prophet ﷺ said, "O Jibra'il, how can the loan be more meritorious than charity?" He replied, "Because the one asking for charity may still have something, while the borrower does not borrow except out of need."

### The Gift of Salah

"After the seventh heaven Jibra'il ascended with him (the Prophet ﷺ) for a distance above that, the distance of which only

Allah ﷻ knows, till he reached the Lote-tree (beyond which none may pass) and then the Irresistible, the Lord of Honour and Majesty approached and came closer till he (Jibra'il) was about two bow lengths or (even) nearer. Among the things which Allah ﷻ revealed to him then, was, 'Fifty prayers were enjoined on his followers in a day and a night.'

"Then the Prophet ﷺ descended and reached Musa عليه السلام who asked, 'What did you do, O Muhammad? What obligations did your Lord impose on you and your Community?' He replied, 'He imposed fifty prayers every day and night on me and my Community.' Musa عليه السلام said, 'Return to your Lord and ask Him to lighten your burden and that of your Community for in truth your Community will not be able to carry it. Verily I myself have experienced people's natures before you. I tested the Children of Israel and took the greatest pains to hold them to something easier than this, but they were too weak to carry it and they abandoned it. Your Community are even weaker in their bodies and constitutions, in their hearts, in their sight, and in their hearing.'

"The Prophet ﷺ turned to Jibra'il to consult him. The latter indicated to him that yes, if you wish, then return. The Prophet ﷺ hurried back until he reached the Tree and the cloud cloaked him and he fell prostrate. Then he said, 'Lord, make lighter the burden of my Community for verily they are the weakest of all Communities.' He replied, 'I have removed five prayers from their obligation.'

"Then the cloud was dispelled and the Prophet ﷺ returned to Musa عليه السلام and told him, 'He has removed five prayers from my obligation.' He replied, 'Go back to your Lord and ask him to make it less, for in truth your Community will not be able to carry that.' The Prophet ﷺ did not cease to go back and forth between Musa عليه السلام and his Lord, while Allah ﷻ each time reduced it by five prayers, until Allah ﷻ said, 'O Muhammad!' The Prophet ﷺ said, 'At Your service, O Lord!' He said, 'Let them be five prayers every day and night, and let every prayer count as ten. That makes fifty prayers. This word of Mine shall not be changed nor shall My Book be abrogated. Let whoever is about to perform a good deed, even if he does not ultimately do it, receive the reward of doing it, while if he does it, he shall receive it tenfold. Let whoever is about to commit a bad deed, and he does not ultimately do it, let not anything be written against him, while if he does it, let one misdeed be written against him.'

"Then the cloud was dispelled and the Prophet ﷺ returned to Musa عليه السلام and told him, 'He has removed five prayers from my obligation.' He replied, 'Go back to your Lord and ask him to make it less, for in truth your Community will not be able to carry that.' The Prophet ﷺ said, 'I have gone back again and again to my Lord now I feel shy. Rather, I accept and submit.'(At this a herald called out, 'I have decreed My obligation and have reduced the burden of My servants.') Musa عليه السلام then said to the Prophet ﷺ, 'Go down in the name of Allah.'"

## The Gift of Surah al-Fatihah

Surah al-Fatihah has seven verses and it has been reported that this is the first surah that was revealed to the Prophet ﷺ in its complete form. It is known by various names including Umm al-Kitab (the Mother of the Book) and Umm al-Qurʾan (essence or mother of the Qurʾan); Imam al-Qurtubi (Allah have mercy on him) has annoted 12 names to this surah. Abu Hurayrah ؓ reports he heard the Prophet ﷺ say, "*Al-Hamdu li Llahi Rabbi l-ʿAlamin* is the mother of the Qurʾan, the mother of the Book and of the seven oft-repeated verses of the glorious Qurʾan."[10]

Kaʿb ؓ reports that the Prophet ﷺ said, "By Him in whose hand is my soul! Allah ﷻ has never revealed in the Tawrah, the Injil, the Zabur or the Furqan a surah like it. It is the seven oft-repeated verses that I was given."[11]

The Holy Prophet ﷺ has also reported that Surah al-Fatihah is a cure for all kinds of illness. According to another narration the surah has also been named the "cure" (al-shifaʾ);[12] and Bukhari reports from Anas ؓ that the Prophet ﷺ has called this surah the greatest among all the surahs of the Holy Qurʾan.

Bukhari, on the authority of Abu Saʿid ibn al-Mualla ﷺ reports that the Prophet ﷺ said, "I will teach you a surah that is the greatest of surahs in the Holy Qurʾan: it is the seven oft-recited verses."

Ibn ʿAbbas ﷺ said, "While Jibraʾil was sitting with the Prophet ﷺ, he heard a sound above him and he raised his head. He said, 'This is a door of heaven which has been opened today and which has never been opened before today. An angel descended from it.' He continued, 'This is an angel who has descended to earth who has never descended before today.' He gave the greeting and said, 'Give the good news of two lights which you have been given and which no Prophet before you was given: the Fatihah of the Book and the end of Surah al-Baqarah. You will not recite a letter of them without being given it.'"[13]

Perhaps the most important *ibadah* or worship of a Muslim is the salah, and Surah al-Fatihah is known as "salah", for reciting it is a condition for prayer to be accepted. Abu Hurayrah ﷺ reports that the Prophet ﷺ said, "Whoever performs any prayer in which he did not read Umm al-Qurʾan (Surah al-Fatihah), then his prayer is incomplete." He said it thrice.[14]

Abu Hurayrah ﷺ reports that the Prophet ﷺ said, "Allah the exalted said, 'I have divided the prayer (al-Fatihah) into two halves between Me and My servant. A half of it is for Me and a half for My servant, and My servant shall acquire what he asked for.' If he says,

'All praise and thanks be to Allah, the Lord of existence,' - Allah ﷻ says, 'My servant has praised Me.'

When the servant says, 'The Most Gracious, the Most Merciful' – Allah ﷻ says, 'My servant has glorified Me.'

When he says, 'Master of the Day of Judgment,' - Allah ﷻ says, 'My servant has glorified Me.'

When he says, 'You (alone) we worship, and You (alone) we ask for help,' - Allah ﷻ says, 'This is between Me and My servant, and My servant shall acquire what he sought.'"

The virtues are further extended when a person says "Amin" after finishing the recitation of Surah al-Fatihah; regarding this the Prophet ﷺ said, "When any of you says in the prayer 'Amin', the angels in the heaven say, 'Amin', in unison, and his previous sins will be forgiven."[15]

### The Gift of the Last Verses of Surah al-Baqarah

Allah ﷻ has completed Surah al-Baqarah with two such verses (i.e. from 2:285 - *Aa-manar-rasoolu bimaa un-zila ilayhi mir-rab-biheewal-mu'-minoon... till the end*) that the Prophet ﷺ said: "[They] have been given to me from the treasures kept beneath the Throne; so learn them and teach them to your wives and children for they are a source of mercy, a form of recitation and prayers."

ءَامَنَ ٱلرَّسُولُ بِمَآ أُنزِلَ إِلَيْهِ مِن رَّبِّهِ وَٱلْمُؤْمِنُونَ كُلٌّ ءَامَنَ بِٱللَّهِ وَمَلَٰٓئِكَتِهِۦ وَكُتُبِهِۦ وَرُسُلِهِۦ لَا نُفَرِّقُ بَيْنَ أَحَدٍ مِّن رُّسُلِهِۦ وَقَالُوا۟ سَمِعْنَا وَأَطَعْنَا غُفْرَانَكَ رَبَّنَا وَإِلَيْكَ ٱلْمَصِيرُ ۝ لَا يُكَلِّفُ ٱللَّهُ نَفْسًا إِلَّا وُسْعَهَا لَهَا مَا كَسَبَتْ وَعَلَيْهَا مَا ٱكْتَسَبَتْ رَبَّنَا لَا تُؤَاخِذْنَآ إِن نَّسِينَآ أَوْ أَخْطَأْنَا رَبَّنَا وَلَا تَحْمِلْ عَلَيْنَآ إِصْرًا كَمَا حَمَلْتَهُۥ عَلَى ٱلَّذِينَ مِن قَبْلِنَا رَبَّنَا وَلَا تُحَمِّلْنَا مَا لَا طَاقَةَ لَنَا بِهِۦ وَٱعْفُ عَنَّا وَٱغْفِرْ لَنَا وَٱرْحَمْنَآ أَنتَ مَوْلَىٰنَا فَٱنصُرْنَا عَلَى ٱلْقَوْمِ ٱلْكَٰفِرِينَ ۝

*The Messenger believes in what has been revealed to him by his Lord, and so do all the believers. Each one of them believes in Allah, His angels, His Books and His Messengers. We make no distinction between any of His Messengers. And they say, "We hear and we obey. Grant us Your forgiveness, our Lord; to You we shall all return." Allah does not charge a soul with more than it can bear. It shall be rewarded for whatever good it does and shall be responsible for whatever evil it does. Our Lord, do not take us to task if we forget or err. Our Lord, do not lay on us a burden such as that You laid on those before us. Our Lord, do not burden us with what we do not have the strength to bear. Pardon us and forgive us our sins and bestow Your Mercy on us. You are our Supreme Lord; grant us victory against the unbelievers. Al-Baqarah 2:285–6*

Reciting from *Amana r-Rasulu...* till the end of the surah will prevent Shaytan from coming even near one's house.

As mentioned earlier, Ibn 'Abbas ﷺ narrates, "While the Prophet ﷺ was sitting with Jibra'il, he heard a voice from above, and raised his head. Then he said, 'That is the door of heaven, opened today, which was never opened before.' And an angel descended from it, and he said, 'That is an angel come down to earth who never came down before.' And he gave a greeting and said, 'Receive good news of two lights brought to you, which never before were brought to a Prophet: Fatihah al-Kitab and the last verses (khawatim) of Surah al-Baqarah; of these thou shalt never recite a single letter without being granted thy request.'"[16]

Abu Musa ﷺ reports that the Prophet ﷺ said, "Whoever recites the last two verses of Surah al-Baqarah at night, they will suffice for him."

[Sahih Bukhari]

It is reported on the authority of Ibn Mas'ud ﷺ that the Prophet ﷺ said, "Whoever recites the last two verses of Surah al-Baqarah at night, they will be sufficient for him."

[Sahih Bukhari]

It is reported on the authority of Abu Dharr ﷺ that the Messenger of Allah ﷺ said, "I was given the final verses of Surah al-Baqarah from a treasure trove beneath the Throne; no Prophet before me was given them."

[Ahmad]

It is reported from 'Uqbah ibn 'Amir al-Juhani ﷺ that Allah's Messenger ﷺ said, "Recite the last two verses from Surah al-Baqarah, for I was given them from a treasure trove beneath the Throne."

[Ahmad]

## The Gift of Pardoning Sins

'Abdullah ibn Mas'ud ⏺ reports, "When the Messenger of Allah ⏺ was taken for the Night Journey, he was taken to Sidrat al-Muntaha, which is situated on the sixth heaven, where everything that ascends from the earth and descends from above it (and is held there) terminates. It is with reference to this that Allah ⏺ said, *'When that which covers, covered the Lote-tree'* (al-Najm 50:16). The Messenger of Allah ⏺ was given three (things): The five prayers; the concluding verses of Surah al-Baqarah; and remission of serious sins for those among his Ummah who do not associate anything with Allah."[17]

This means that members of the Ummah will not suffer eternal punishment on account of their major sins, but will instead be pardoned either through repentance and seeking the forgiveness of Allah ⏺, or after first being punished for their sins.[18]

# 8 | The Descent and Return to Makkah

THE PROPHET ﷺ having experienced the 'heavens', was once again brought down to Masjid al-Aqsa. Once there he mounted the Buraq, which had been tied to what is now called the Buraq (Western) Wall and made his way back to Makkah. He passed by a caravan of the Quraysh on the way (the narrator forgot the name of the place) and saw a camel upon which were tied two containers, a black one and a white one. When he came face to face with the caravan there was a stampede in which the caravan turned around and the camel was thrown down to the ground and its cargo broke free.

Then the Prophet ﷺ passed by another caravan which had lost one of their camels (and which a certain tribe had rounded up). The Prophet ﷺ greeted them and one of the men said, "This is the voice of Muhammad!" After that, the Prophet ﷺ returned to Makkah. All of this, al-Isra' and al-Mi'raj, took place in one special night.

When morning came Prophet Muhammad ﷺ made his way towards the Ka'bah. In one narration it states that his cousin Umm Hani (who was a Muslim) was the first to be informed about the journey he had made. She accepted the Prophet's ﷺ experience but as the Prophet ﷺ was making his way to the Ka'bah she requested, "I fear that the people would not believe you if you tell them what you have just told me." The Prophet ﷺ made clear his intention to tell them even though they would not believe him.[1]

While the Prophet ﷺ was sitting next to the Ka'bah it was an irony of fate that the first person he met was Abu Jahl, the arch enemy of Islam; a man dedicated to undermining and silencing the Prophet ﷺ. Mockingly he asked Prophet Muhammad ﷺ, "Have you any news today?" The Prophet ﷺ replied, "Yes." Abu Jahl said, "And what is that?" The Prophet ﷺ replied, "Last night I was taken to Jerusalem." Abu Jahl was amazed; he asked again, "To where?" The Prophet ﷺ replied, "To Jerusalem." Abu Jahl asked, "Then you woke up here among us?" He ﷺ replied, "Yes."

Abu Jahl sensed an opportunity to drive a wedge between the Makkans and the Prophet ﷺ so said, "If I call the others to come over, would you repeat to them what you have just told me?" Unhesitatingly, the Prophet ﷺ replied, "Yes."

Abu Jahl called out ecstatically to as many people as he could and soon the gathering became a small crowd. He turned to the Prophet ﷺ and said, "Tell your people what you just told me." The Prophet ﷺ repeated, "Last night I was taken to Jerusalem." They said, "Then you woke up here among us?" He replied, "Yes." The people were incredulous and sceptical They expressed their disbelief by putting their hands over their mouths and heads.

As his ﷺ account of the journey was completed many rushed around Makkah relating the fantastic "claim" made by the Prophet ﷺ. Some, thinking this was an opportunity to distance Abu Bakr ؓ from the Prophet ﷺ, went in search of him. Abu Bakr's response was profound; upon hearing their account he stated, "If he [the Prophet ﷺ] has actually said this, he is telling the truth." The people began to express amazement that he could believe such a story. Abu Bakr ؓ said, "What is so surprising? I believe him when he says something even more incomprehensible, that he receives revelations from Allah ﷻ."[2]

Abu Bakr ؓ then followed the few who had come to him to the Ka'bah where people still gathered around the Prophet ﷺ and were questioning him about his story.

Upon meeting the Prophet ﷺ Abu Bakr ؓ asked him if he had said what the people were reporting. The Prophet ﷺ said, "Yes." Abu Bakr ؓ immediately, without hesitating, responded: "I believe you; you always tell the truth." The people around began to ask the Prophet ﷺ to describe Jerusalem to them and for every response the Prophet ﷺ made, Abu Bakr ؓ kept on repeating, "I believe you; you always tell the truth." The Prophet ﷺ appreciated Abu Bakr's trust, at a time when most disbelieved him, and gave him the title Siddiq, which denotes "a true believer" (or, "the one who affirms the truth"). This title remained with Abu Bakr ؓ throughout his lifetime and it will be so until the end of time.

> Jābir ibn ʿAbdullāh ؓ relates that the Prophet ﷺ said, "When the people of Quraysh did not believe me (i.e. the story of my Night Journey), I stood up in al-Hijr and Allah ﷻ displayed Bayt al-Maqdis (Jerusalem) in front of me, and I began describing it to them while I was looking at it."
>
> [Ṣaḥīḥ al-Bukhārī]

Then they said, "O Muhammad, tell us about our caravans." He ﷺ replied, "I saw the caravan of the tribe of so-and-so as I was coming back. They had lost one of their camels and were searching for it everywhere. I reached their mounts and there was no one with them. I found a water bottle and I drank from it."

The Prophet ﷺ continued, "Then I reached the caravan of the tribe of so-and-so in such-and-such a place. I saw a red camel carrying one black container and one white one. When I came face to face with the caravan there was a stampede and a camel fell and its cargo broke. Then I reached the caravan (not previously mentioned) of the tribe of so-and-so in al-Tanʿim. It was headed by a greyish camel on which was a black hair-cloth and two blackish containers and here are the (three) caravans about to reach you from the mountain pass." They said, "When will they arrive?" He replied, "On the fourth day of the week." On that day the Quraysh came out, expecting the caravans.

The day passed and they did not arrive. The Prophet ﷽ made an invocation and the day was extended one more hour during which the sun stood still, and the caravans came.

They went to meet the riders and asked them, "Did you lose a camel?" They said yes. They asked the second caravan, "Did one red camel of yours shatter her freight?" They said, "Yes." They asked (the first caravan), "Did anyone lose a water bottle?" One man said, "I did, by Allah, I had prepared it but none of us drank it nor was it spilled on the ground!" At this point they accused the Prophet ﷽ of sorcery and they said, "al-Walid spoke the truth."[3] And Allah ﷽ revealed the verse,

$$وَإِذْ قُلْنَا لَكَ إِنَّ رَبَّكَ أَحَاطَ بِالنَّاسِ وَمَا جَعَلْنَا الرُّؤْيَا الَّتِي أَرَيْنَاكَ إِلَّا فِتْنَةً لِّلنَّاسِ وَالشَّجَرَةَ الْمَلْعُونَةَ فِي الْقُرْآنِ وَنُخَوِّفُهُمْ فَمَا يَزِيدُهُمْ إِلَّا طُغْيَانًا كَبِيرًا ۝$$

*We said to you that your Lord encompasses all mankind. We have made the vision which we have shown you, as also the tree cursed in this Qur'an, only a trial for people. We seek to put fear in their hearts, but it only increases their gross transgression.*

(Al-Isra' 17:60)

The supernatural events which took place at the time of the Prophet ﷽, such as his Night Journey, were not meant as proof of his message. These were given as a test for his people.

Some of those who believed in the message preached by the Prophet ﷽ reverted to unbelief after he told them about his Night Journey. Others, however, became firmer than ever in their belief. Hence, it is true that what Allah ﷽ showed His Messenger on that night was meant as "a trial for men" so that they would affirm their faith.

The Prophet ﷽ told his people of Allah's promise and what he had seen. This included the tree of Zaqqum which grows in hell. It is a tree which Allah ﷽ cites as a warning to unbelievers. However, they continued to deny the message and all that the Prophet ﷺ said. Abu Jahl, the arch-enemy of Islam, even ridiculed the tree, playing on the sense given by its name. He asked for dates and butter and mixed them together and ate them. He said to those around, "Come and eat, this is the only Zaqqum we know."[4]

The *mushrikīn* (idol worshippers) like many today, did not believe the truth and they rushed back to Prophet Muḥammad ﷺ and began to quiz him about his journey. The ḥadīth states:

> "I had never before been as uneasy as I was at the time they interrogated me. Though I had seen Bayt al-Maqdis (Jerusalem) in al-Isra', I could not recollect in detail the exact description. However, Allah ﷻ revealed before my very eyes an image of Bayt al-Maqdis (Jerusalem) and thereafter I was immediately able to answer the questions the Quraysh of Makkah asked me."
>
> [Ṣaḥīḥ Muslim]

# 9 | The Significance of al-Isra'

AL-ISRA' IS the defining moment for Muslims in emphasizing the significance of Jerusalem. It is a clear indication that Allah ﷻ chose Jerusalem over any other place on earth from which to take the Prophet ﷺ on the Night Journey. More specifically, He ﷻ could have taken the Prophet ﷺ directly from Makkah to the heavens but instead He chose this city which He has blessed. Thus, it should become apparent to the Ummah that Jerusalem holds *barakah* or blessings and this should remain at the forefront of our minds. It is also of note that Jerusalem did not become important to Muslims because of the Night Journey but rather the Prophet ﷺ was taken via Jerusalem because of its prior importance. Jerusalem is thus eternally tied to the consciousness of the believers.

The taking of the Noble Prophet ﷺ to Jerusalem indicates several factors:

1. This was to link the first Masjid built on earth, the Ka'bah, with the second Masjid built on earth, Masjid al-Aqsa.
2. During the Night Journey, the Prophet ﷺ became the imam of the two Blessed sites of the Ka'bah and al-Aqsa, when neither were under his control. This was to show the Islamic heritage of both of these cities and the need to bring them under Islamic rule. Events led first to Makkah being liberated and, in 17AH/637CE, Jerusalem being liberated.
3. The ascent of the Prophet ﷺ beyond the Sidrat al-Muntaha, where even Jibra'il could not go, is a clear indication of his high status.

The Prophet's ﷺ presence in the court of the Almighty stamped the authority of his closeness to Allah ﷻ and the responsibility of this Ummah.

4. The Night Journey binds the Ummah to the two qiblahs which were united through this journey. The Muslims' first qiblah (the direction in which to face when in prayer) for approximately 14 years was Jerusalem, and thereafter it has been the Ka'bah. It is no coincidence that these two holy places were linked through the Prophet's ﷺ journey via Jerusalem.

5. It also serves to link the universal significance of the Prophet ﷺ, the Ka'bah and Jerusalem. The Holy Qur'an, referring to the Prophet ﷺ states, "We have not sent you, but as a mercy for all beings" (wa ma arsalnaka illa rahmahtan lil'alamin). (21:107) It further refers to the Ka'bah as "Full of blessing and of guidance for all kinds of beings", (3:96) and to Jerusalem as the "land which We have blessed for all people". (21:71) Al-Isra' bound the Prophet ﷺ and these two holy places together during this one great night.

6. In addition, with regard to the route of the journey from Makkah to Jerusalem, Ahmad Rabi' Yusuf argues that it has a special significance. Yusuf argues that the journey "went through all the places where a revelation has been brought to earth throughout history; it started from Makkah, where the revelation to Muhammad ﷺ started, and went by Madinah, in which the revelation continued to Muhammad ﷺ, then it passed near Sinai, where Musa ﷺ had the revelation, and it ended where the revelation came to Zachariah ﷺ, Isa ﷺ, Dawud ﷺ and Sulayman ﷺ". This argument is very interesting since it connects the final element in the study of the significance of the place, namely the route. This link is also made in the Qur'an (95: 1–3), where Allah ﷻ takes an oath by three places, Jerusalem, Sinai, and Makkah.[1]

وَٱلتِّينِ وَٱلزَّيْتُونِ ۞ وَطُورِ سِينِينَ ۞ وَهَـٰذَا ٱلْبَلَدِ ٱلْأَمِينِ ۞ لَقَدْ خَلَقْنَا ٱلْإِنسَـٰنَ فِى
أَحْسَنِ تَقْوِيمٍ ۞ ثُمَّ رَدَدْنَـٰهُ أَسْفَلَ سَـٰفِلِينَ ۞

*By the Fig and the Olive, And the Mount of Sinai, And this City of
security, We have indeed created man in the best of moulds, then do
We abase him (to be) the lowest of the low.*

(Al-Tīn 95:1–5)

The events that took place in al-Aqsa are of profound importance
and further show the magnitude of al-Isra' and the significance of
Jerusalem:

1. The Prophet ﷺ led the salah in al-Aqsa with all the other
   Messengers of Allah ﷻ who have been sent to earth praying
   behind him. This historic and exclusive event, the only one of its
   kind to our knowledge, placed the Prophet ﷺ as the leader of the
   Prophets ﷺ. This honourable elevation of the Prophet ﷺ adds
   a significant dimension to both our understanding of Jerusalem
   and al-Isra'.

2. Al-Aqsa became the only known site on the entire planet where all
   the Prophets and the Messengers ﷺ performed salah together
   at one given time, led by the final Prophet Muhammad ﷺ.

3. It is extremely significant that Allah ﷻ assembled all the Prophets
   and Messengers in Jerusalem, as this indicates the inclusiveness
   of Islam, whereby Islam does not undermine nor differentiate
   between the Prophets and Messengers. In fact, the Qur'an says:

قُولُوٓا۟ ءَامَنَّا بِٱللَّهِ وَمَآ أُنزِلَ إِلَيْنَا وَمَآ أُنزِلَ إِلَىٰٓ إِبْرَٰهِـۧمَ وَإِسْمَـٰعِيلَ وَإِسْحَـٰقَ وَيَعْقُوبَ
وَٱلْأَسْبَاطِ وَمَآ أُوتِىَ مُوسَىٰ وَعِيسَىٰ وَمَآ أُوتِىَ ٱلنَّبِيُّونَ مِن رَّبِّهِمْ لَا نُفَرِّقُ بَيْنَ أَحَدٍ مِّنْهُمْ
وَنَحْنُ لَهُۥ مُسْلِمُونَ ۞

*Say! We believe in Allah and the revelation given to Ibrahim, Isma'il, Ishaq, Ya'qub and the tribes. And that given to Musa and 'Isa and that given to all Prophets from their Lord. We make no distinction between one and another of them and we bow to Allah (in Islam).*
(Al-Baqarah 2:136)

4. The presence of all the Prophets and Prophet Muhammad ﷺ leading the salaah also indicates the finality of Allah's ﷻ message to humanity. On this night, while all the Prophets and Messengers respected the leadership of Prophet Muhammad ﷺ, he ﷺ was also acknowledged as being the final Messenger, whose responsibility it was to complete the message that had begun with Adam ﷺ.

5. The fact that Allah ﷻ chose to make al-Aqṣā a station in this incredible journey is worthy of note; and it must be recalled that Prophet Muḥammad ﷺ not only stopped at al-Aqṣā on his journey from Makkah to the Sublime Throne, but he also stopped there on the return journey. The visit of the Prophet ﷺ to Jerusalem before returning to Makkah adds permanency to the importance of Jerusalem and al-Aqsa. This undermines the arguments of those who contend that the importance of Jerusalem ceased after the ascension. This fact indicates the importance of Jerusalem until the end of time for the believers.

6. Besides al-Aqsa being a station in the Night Journey, the fact that such major events took place there rather than anywhere else highlights the primacy of al-Aqsa.

# 10 | Conclusion

AL-ISRA' AND AL-MI'RAJ were not miracles to prove the prophet-hood of Muhammad ﷺ; rather they represent an incredible journey of tremendous importance undertaken by Prophet Muhammad ﷺ through the power of Allah ﷻ. It was the highest accolade afforded to the Prophet ﷺ. He undertook a journey no other human has been able to make, on a mode of transport that was only accessible to the greatest of the previous Prophets. Those who have faith in Allah ﷻ have no hesitation in accepting the Night Journey, as Allah ﷻ is Supreme with power above all things.

The timing of al-Isra' is also significant in relation to both the Prophet's ﷺ mission and status amongst his contemporaries. As mentioned earlier this was the time when he was least secure, most prone to attacks and gravely concerned about the future of his mission. However, through the Night Journey Allah ﷻ empowered him and indicated the futility of those rebels on earth who were presenting obstacles to the mission. The solace and comfort the Prophet ﷺ gained from this journey almost mid-way in his ﷺ prophethood was absolute.

The Islamic creed is set apart from the other monotheistic faiths for a number of reasons, most pertinently due to the fact that the Ummah, through the will of Allah ﷻ, has preserved in great detail the actual and specific words spoken by Prophet Muhammad ﷺ, the final Messenger to humanity, with full chains of narrators whose authenticity has been verified painstakingly. It is only Muslims who can claim this, since no words attributed to 'Isa ﷺ or Musa ﷺ

(outside of the Qur'an) claimed by the Christians or Jews can be verified or proven to have actually been uttered by the respective Prophets. Again, it is only Muslims who can testify to have received the words from Ibrahim 🕊, Musa 🕊 and 'Isa 🕊 without any doubt. The ahadith about the Night Journey are quoted directly from Prophet Muhammad 🕊 regarding his conversations and, on occasion, the advice he 🕊 received from the aforementioned Prophets. Hence, al-Isra' and al-Mi'raj provided Muslims with a magnanimous bounty, and that was the opportunity to received unadulterated messages from those great Prophets.

The Prophet's 🕊 faith was immovable but became secured even further by the Might of Allah 🕊 and this journey nurtured him and enabled him to face every conceivable challenge. The greatness of the physical journey itself pales into insignificance when contrasted to the depth and breadth of experiences he encountered and the meetings he had during al-Mi'raj. To see and meet previous Prophets and the angels is not insignificant, and to have been greeted by them and showered with respect is without doubt one of the most honourable experiences of the Prophet 🕊. This helped to banish the anguish created by the taunts and obstinacy of the tribe of Quraish.

The appointment of Prophet Muhammad 🕊 as the imam of all the Prophets when he led the prayers within al-Aqsa cannot be underestimated. It was an honour of majestic proportions, especially when one considers that the Prophet 🕊 was leading all the Prophets including the first man on earth, our and his 🕊 father Adam 🕊 and the other great Prophets like Ibrahim 🕊, Musa 🕊, Dawud 🕊 and 'Isa 🕊. This appointment of authority should be seen in its correct perspective, as a mighty responsibility and an indication of the finality of Prophethood and the transfer of Allah's message to the final Prophet, Muhammad 🕊. His 🕊 subsequent meetings with the principle Prophets during various stages of the journey was a source of comfort and reassurance from his Prophetic "brothers and father". He 🕊 was able to draw strength from their experiences and witness the true life of the Hereafter which awakened him 🕊 to the responsibility of his ﷺ own mission which was yet to be completed.

Witnessing the reality of the hereafter with both heaven and hell being unfolded in front of his ﷺ eyes must have strengthened him immeasurably in his ﷺ mission, driving him ﷺ to leave no stone unturned when warning humanity about the perils of going astray.

The greatest bounty of all was his ﷺ being taken to the presence of Allah Almighty, the Lord ﷻ of the Worlds. Prophet Muhammad ﷺ was allowed to ascend where no other had or has been allowed to, not even angel Jibra'il. This audience was not restricted to one visit, but following the advice of Musa ﷺ, he ﷺ asked again and again for Allah ﷻ to reduce the number of obligatory prayers. In this way, Prophet Muhammad ﷺ was able to meet Allah ﷻ, the Most Gracious, the Most Merciful, the Lord of All the Worlds, the Limitless, the Magnificent, ten times.

If one considers the life of this world and all of its frailties, trials, tribulations and hardships and one remembers that these are tests set by Allah ﷻ Most High, in order to separate the righteous from those who go astray, what greater bounty could He ﷻ bestow on His servants than to grant them an audience? Only Prophet Muhammad ﷺ has been worthy of this glory. The exclusive audience with Allah ﷻ washed away all of his ﷺ sorrows and concerns, instilling in him a renewed determination to dedicate himself with ardent vigour towards his central purpose of delivering the Message and reforming humanity across the world.

After considering the greatness and significance of al-Isra' and al-Mi'raj it is not surprising to understand how it impacted on the course of history. Prior to the Night Journey, the Prophet ﷺ was fighting for his ﷺ own survival. After this incredible journey, he ﷺ returned to his mission with unbending faith and renewed vigour. A few months after this event, the Prophet ﷺ undertook the Hijrah (Emigration) to Madinah, and thereafter victory followed victory. The Prophet ﷺ established an Islamic state, something that appeared inconceivable just a few months earlier. His ﷺ Companions also benefitted by being imbibed with resolute conviction in both their faith and their mission. The once sworn enemies and doubters of this very journey in time embraced faith sincerely and the numbers of the faithful began to grow exponentially.

Allah ﷻ the Most High, the best of planners, raised the Prophet ﷺ to Him ﷻ and showed him ﷺ the reality of this transitory world during the incredible Night Journey. In this are lessons for us all, and a reminder. The life of this world is nothing but a gilded cage, and if we are distracted by what is apparent here on earth, we will surely lose out on the promises of an everlasting paradise. Besides al-Isra' and al-Mi'raj having enriched the Prophet ﷺ they provided the ummah with an eyewitness account from the most reliable source of the future which all of creation will have to encounter. Remembrance of this great journey strengthens the *Iman* of the believer in the hereafter and thereby plays a pivotal role in ensuring good conduct during his lifetime on earth. The event became a means through which the course of history changed for the Prophet ﷺ and for Islam. For the believers who ponder over this journey, its impact should be no less, insha'Allah.

# Appendix 1

### Fasting in Rajab and Sha'ban

'Abd al-Rahman al-Jaza'iri[1]: Fasting the months of Rajab and Sha'ban is recommended (*mandub*) as agreed upon by three of the Imams, while the Hanbalis differed in that they said fasting in Rajab singly is disliked, except if one breaks the fast during it then it is not disliked. Regarding the holy months - Dhul Qa'da, Dhul Hijjah, Muharram and Rajab - fasting in them is recommended according to three of the Imams, while the Hanafis differed in that they said what is recommended in the Holy months is to fast three days from each of them, which are Thursday, Friday and Saturday.

> Muslim, Abu Dawud, and Ahmad relate that 'Uthman ibn Hakim al-Ansari ﷺ said, "I asked Sa'id ibn Jubayr ﷺ about fasting in Rajab, and we were then passing through the month of Rajab, whereupon he said, 'I heard Ibn 'Abbas ﷺ saying, "The Messenger of Allah ﷺ used to observe fast so continuously that we thought he would never break it, and at other times he remained without fasting so continuously that we thought he would never fast."[2]

Imam al-Nawawi comments: "It appears that the meaning inferred by Sa'id ibn Jubayr ﷺ from Ibn 'Abbas's report is that fasting in Rajab is neither forbidden nor considered praiseworthy in itself; rather, the ruling concerning it is the same as the rest of the months. Neither prohibition nor praiseworthiness has been established for the month of Rajab in itself; however, the principle concerning fasting is that it is praiseworthy in itself, and in the *Sunan* of Abu Dawud[3] the Prophet has made the fasting of the sacred months praiseworthy, and Rajab is one of them. And Allah knows best."[4]

> Muslim, Ibn Majah, and Ahmad (to some extent) relate that 'Abdullah, the freed slave of Asma' the daughter of Abu Bakr ﷺ, the maternal uncle of the son of 'Ata', reported, Asma' sent me to 'Abdullah ibn 'Umar ﷺ saying, "The news has reached me that you prohibit the use of three things, the striped robe, saddle cloth made of red silk, and fasting the whole month of Rajab." Abdullah ﷺ said to me, "So far as what you say about fasting in the month of Rajab, how about one who observes continuous fasting? And so far as what you say about the striped garment, I heard 'Umar ibn al-Khattab ﷺ say that he had heard from Allah's Messenger ﷺ, 'He who wears a silk garment, has no share (in the Hereafter).' And I am afraid that stripes were part of it. And so far as the red saddle cloth is concerned, here is 'Abdullah's saddle cloth and it is red." I went back to Asma' and informed her, so she said, "Here is the cloak (*jubbah*) of Allah's Messenger ﷺ," and she brought out to me that cloak made of Persian cloth with a hem of (silk) brocade, and its sleeves bordered with (silk) brocade, and said, "This was Allah's Messenger's ﷺ cloak with 'A'ishah until she died, then I took possession of it. The Messenger of Allah used to wear that, and we washed it for the sick so that they could seek cure with it."[5]

Al-Nawawi commented on the above: Ibn 'Umar's reply concerning fasting in Rajab is a denial on his part of what Asma' had heard with regard to his forbidding it, and it is an affirmation that he fasted Rajab in its entirety as well as fasting permanently, i.e. except the days of Eid and *tashriq*.[6] This (perpetual fast) is his way and the way of his father 'Umar ibn al-Khattab, 'A'ishah, Abu Talhah, and others of the pious predecessors (salaf), as well as al-Shafi'i and other scholars, their position being that perpetual fasting is not disliked (makruh).

> Abu Dawud and Bayhaqi, from Mujibah al-Bahiliyyah, who reported that her father or uncle was told by the Prophet ﷺ three times, "Fast some and leave some in the sacred months."[7]

> In Muslim from Abu Hurayrah, The best month to fast after Ramadan is Muharram.

As for hafiz Ibn Hajar's opinion, it only applies to the pure singling out of the month of Rajab at the exclusion of Ramadan, or Sha'ban, or the sacred months, or the rest of the entire year, which does not have a basis. But his opinion does not provide a basis for the claim of the objectors that fasting during Rajab is forbidden or that it is an innovation, for neither the Imams of the fours schools, nor Bayhaqi, nor al-Nawawi, nor Ibn Hajar, nor even Sayyid Sabiq have claimed this! Furthermore, there is also no sound hadith from the Prophet ﷺ forbidding the fast of Rajab or disavowing its merit.

a. As for those who object by quoting the hadith in *Bukhari* and *Muslim* whereby the Prophet ﷺ emphasized that the one who fasts all his life has not fasted, then their understanding of this hadith is diametrically opposed to that of the Companions and the pious predecessors (salaf), Abu Hanifah, Malik, al-Shafi'i, and Ahmad, who did not dislike perpetual fasting as long as it did not include the days of Eid and *tashriq*.

b. As for the narration from Ibn 'Abbas ؓ whereby the Prophet ﷺ forbade the fast of Rajab, then only Ibn Majah reports it, with a chain containing Dawud ibn 'Ata' al-Muzani concerning whom Buhakri, Ibn Abu Hatim, and Abu Zur'ah said, "His hadith is rejected (*munkar al-hadith*)," and al-Nasa'i declared him weak (*da'if*), and Ahmad said, "He is nothing." The chain also contains

Abu Ayyub Sulayman ibn 'Ali al-Hashimi about whom Yahya ibn Sa'id al-Qattan said, "His case is not known," although Ibn Hibban declared him trustworthy, but Ibn Hibban's leniency in this is known.

In conclusion, it is at the very least permissible to fast Rajab and Sha'ban in part or in whole, and we say it is recommended, as the clarity of the intention to follow the sunnah and the knowledge that only the fast of Ramadan is obligatory, preclude the reprehensibility of those who used to honour Rajab in rivalry with Ramadan. Sufficient proof of the month of Rajab's status as a great month lies in the fact that it is the month of the Prophet's rapture and ascension to his Lord (*al-Isra' wa al-Mi'raj*), and they are blessed who commemorate this month and that night for the sake of Allah's favour to His Prophet ﷺ and the Community of His Prophet ﷺ. And Allah knows best.[8]

# Appendix 2

### Celebrating the Night of Ascension (Laylat al-Mi'raj)

Mufti Taqi Usmani[1] Rajab is the seventh month in the Islamic lunar calendar. This month was regarded as one of the sacred months (al-Ashhur-al-hurum) in which battles were prohibited in the days of the Holy Prophet 鏸. It is also a prelude to the month of Ramadan, because Ramadan follows it after the intervening month of Sha'ban. Therefore, when the Holy Prophet 鏸 sighted the moon of Rajab, he used to pray to Allah 鏸 in the following words:

> "O Allah, make the months of Rajab and Sha'ban blessed for us, and let us reach the month of Ramadan (i.e. prolong our life up to Ramadan, so that we may benefit from its merits and blessings)."

Yet no specific way of worship has been prescribed by the Shari'ah in this month. However, some people have invented some special rituals or practices in this month, which are not supported by reliable resources of the Shari'ah or are based on some unauthentic traditions. We would like to explain here the correct position about them.

Celebration of Laylat al-Mi'raj: It is generally believed that the great event of Mi'raj (ascension of the Holy Prophet 鏸 to the heavens) took place in the night of 27th of Rajab. Therefore, some people celebrate the night as "Laylat al-Mi'raj" (the Night of Ascension to the heavens).

Indeed, the event of Mi'raj was one of the most remarkable episodes in the life of our beloved Holy Prophet 鹵. He was summoned by Almighty Allah 鹵. He travelled from Makkah to Bayt al-Maqdis and from there he ascended the heavens through the miraculous power of Allah 鹵. He was honoured with a direct contact with his Creator at a place where even the angels had no access. This was the unique honour conferred by Allah 鹵 to the Holy Prophet 鹵 alone. It was the climax of the spiritual progress which is not attained by anybody except him. No doubt the night in which he was blessed with this unparalleled honour was one of the greatest nights in the history of this world. But, Islam has its own principles with regard to the historic and religious events. Its approach about observing festivals and celebrating days and nights is totally different from the approach of other religions. The Holy Qur'an and the sunnah of the Holy Prophet did not prescribe any festival or any celebration to commemorate an event from the past, however remarkable it might have been. Instead, Islam has prescribed two annual celebrations only. One is Eid al-Fitr and the other is Eid al-Adha. Both of these festivals have been fixed at a date on which the Muslims accomplish a great 'ibadah (worship) every year. Eid al-Fitr has been prescribed after the fasts of Ramadan, while Eid al-Adha has been fixed when the Muslims perform the Hajj annually. None of these two Eids are designed to commemorate a particular event of the past. This approach is indicative of the fact that the real occasion for a happy celebration is the day in which the celebrators themselves have accomplished remarkable work through their own active effort.

As for the accomplishments of our ancestors, their commemoration should not be restricted to a particular day or night. Instead, their accomplishments must be remembered every day in the practical life by observing their teachings and following the great examples they have set for us. Keeping this principle in view, the following points should be remembered with regard to the "Laylat al-Mi'raj":

1. We cannot say with absolute certainty in which night the great event of al-Mi'raj took place. Although some traditions relate

this event to the 27th night of the month of Rajab, yet there are other traditions that suggest other dates. Al-Zurqani, the famous biographer of the Holy Prophet 🕮 has referred to five different views in this respect, Rabi' al- Awwal, Rabi' al-Thani, Rajab, Ramadan, and Shawwal. Later, while discussing different traditions, he has added a sixth opinion, that the al-Mi'raj took place in the month of Dhul Hijjah.

Allama 'Abd al-Haqq Muhaddith Dehlawi, the well-known scholar of the Indian subcontinent, has written a detailed book on the merits of Islamic months. While discussing the "Laylat al-Mi'raj" he has mentioned that most of the scholars are of the view that the event of al-Mi'raj took place in the month of Ramadan or in Rabi' al-Awwal.

2. It is also not known in which year the event of al-Mi'raj took place. The books of history suggest a wide range between the fifth year to the twelfth year after the Holy Prophet 🕮 was entrusted with Prophethood.

Now, if it is assumed that the event of al-Mi'raj took place in the fifth year of his Prophethood, it will mean that the Holy Prophet 🕮 remained in this world for eighteen years after this event. Even if it is presumed that the al-Mi'raj took place in the twelfth year of his Prophethood, his remaining life-time after this event would be eleven years. Throughout this long period, which may range between eleven years to eighteen years, the Holy Prophet 🕮 never celebrated the event of al-Mi'raj, nor did he give any instruction about it. No one can prove that the Holy Prophet 🕮 ever performed some specific modes of worship in a night, calling it the "Laylat al-Mi'raj" or advised his followers to commemorate the event in a particular manner.

3. After the demise of the Holy Prophet 🕮 also, none of his Companions are reported to have celebrated this night as a night of special acts of worship. They were the true devotees of the Holy Prophet 🕮 and had devoted their lives to preserve every minute detail

of the sunnah of the Holy Prophet ﷺ and other Islamic teachings. Still, they did not celebrate the event of al-Mi'raj in a particular night in a particular way.

All these points go a long way to prove that the celebration of the 27th night of Rajab, being the Laylat al-Mi'raj has no basis in the sunnah of the Holy Prophet ﷺ or in the practice of his noble Companions. Had it been a commendable practice to celebrate this night, the exact date of this event would have been preserved accurately by the Ummah and the Holy Prophet ﷺ and his blessed Companions would have given specific directions for it.

Therefore, it is not a sunnah to celebrate the Laylat al-Mi'raj. We cannot declare any practice as a sunnah unless it is established through authentic sources that the Holy Prophet ﷺ or his noble Companions have recognized as such, otherwise it may become a bid'ah about which the Holy Prophet ﷺ has observed in the following words, "Whoever invents something in our religion which is not a part of it, it is to be rejected."

Being mindful of this serious warning, we should appreciate that the 27th night of the month of Rajab is not like "Laylat al-Qadr" or "Laylat al-Bara'ah" for which special merits have been mentioned expressly either by the Holy Qur'an or by the Holy Prophet ﷺ.

However, all the recognized modes of 'ibadah (worship) like salah, recitation of the Holy Qur'an, dhikr, etc. are commendable at anytime, especially in the late hours of night and obviously the 27th night of Rajab is not an exception. Therefore, if someone performs any recognized 'ibadah in this night from this point of view nothing can stop him from doing so, and he will be entitled to the thawab (reward allocated for that recognized 'ibadah insha-Allah). But it is not permissible to believe that performing 'ibadah in this night is more meritorious or carries more thawab like "Laylat al-Qadr" or "Laylat al-Bara'ah", because this belief is not based on any authentic verse or on a sunnah of the Holy Prophet ﷺ. Similarly, it is not a correct practice to celebrate this night collectively and to invite people to special ritual congregations.

4. Some people suggest some special modes of worship to be performed in this night. Since no special mode of worship is prescribed by the Shari'ah in this night, these suggestions are devoid of any authority and should not be acted upon.

It is believed by some that the Muslims should keep fast on 27th of Rajab. Although there are some traditions attributing special merits to the fast of this day yet the scholars of hadith have held these traditions as very weak and unauthentic reports which cannot be sufficient to establish a rule of Shari'ah. On the contrary, there is an authentic report that 'Umar ﷺ, used to forbid people from fasting on this day, rather to compel them to eat if they had started fasting.

It should be borne in mind here that a 'nafl' fast can be observed any day (except the six prohibited days of the year); therefore, fasting on 27th of Rajab is not prohibited in itself.

What is prohibited is the belief that fasting on this day is more meritorious than fasting in other normal days. One should not fast in this day with this belief. But if someone fasts therein, believing it to be a normal nafl fast, there is no bar against it. Sacrifice (qurbani) in the month of Rajab: in the Days of Ignorance (jahiliyyah) was practiced by the Arabs, who used to offer the sacrifice of a goat in the month of Rajab. This sacrifice used to be called 'Atirah' or 'Rajabiyyah'. This sacrifice was offered in the name of different so-called gods and their icons. In the beginning of Islam, this custom was retained, but the Muslims modified it by offering the sacrifice of 'Atirah' in the name of Allah instead of the false gods. But finally, this custom was abandoned and the Holy Prophet ﷺ prohibited the offering of 'Atirah'. In a tradition of Abu Hurayrah ﷺ, reported by both al-Bukhari and Muslim, the Holy Prophet ﷺ has said, "Fara'is nothing and 'Atirah is nothing."

Abu Hurayrah ﷺ, has explained in the same tradition that Fara' was the first child of a she-camel. Whenever a she-camel delivered its first child, the Arabs used to sacrifice it in the name of their so-called gods, while the 'Atirah was a goat used to be sacrificed in the month of Rajab. Since the Holy Prophet ﷺ stopped both these customs, 'Atirah is no longer a recognized practice.

'Umrah in the month of Rajab Ibn 'Abidin, the well-known scholar of the Islamic jurisprudence, has mentioned that the people of Makkah (in his days) used to perform 'umrah in the month of Rajab. Perhaps they believed that performing 'umrah in this month is more meritorious than in other months. Then Ibn 'Abidin himself has rejected the authenticity of this practice, because no tradition of the Holy Prophet 🌸 is found to this effect. Conversely Sayyidah 'A'ishah, ﷻ, has expressly negated the presumption by saying that the Holy Prophet 🌸 never performed an 'umrah in the month of Rajab (Sahih Muslim 1,409). However, Ibn 'Abidin has quoted a narration that 'Abdullah ibn Zubayr ﷻ, completed the renovation of the Ka'bah shortly before 27th of Rajab, and as a sign of gratefulness he performed 'umrah and slaughtered some animals. But this report cannot form the basis of a recognized annual practice, firstly because the report is not very authentic, and secondly because it does not mention that 'Abdullah ibn Zubayr ﷻ, had adopted it as a continuing practice. At the most, he performed 'umrah once as a sign of gratefulness on the completion of the Ka'bah. It does not mean that he performed it as a characteristic of the month of Rajab. Therefore, performing 'umrah in this month is like performing it in any other month and no special merit can be attached to it merely because it has been performed in the month of Rajab.

## The Salah of Ragha'ib

Another special mode of worship attributed by some people to this month is the Salah of Raghai'b. According to the custom of such people, this Salah is performed in the night of first Friday of the month of Eajab. The Salah of Raghaib is said to consist of twelve rak'ahs [units] to be performed in pairs with six salams, and in each rak'ah the surah al-qadr is recited three times followed by the Surah-al-ikhlas. This type of Salah is also not based on any sound source of Shari'ah. Therefore, almost all the jurists and scholars of Shari'ah have held that the Salah of Raghaib is a baseless practice and it is not permissible to treat it as a recognized practice of this month. It is true that there is a tradition, narrated by Razin, the author of a book of hadith, which attributes the origin of this practice to the Holy Prophet ﷺ but almost all the scholars of the science of hadith have held it to be absolutely unauthentic. Therefore, no importance can be attached to it.

## Distribution of Bread

Another baseless practice in the month of Rajab is that the people bake special types of breads and, after reciting some verses and prayers on them, distribute them among their friends and neighbors. This custom has two different shapes.

In some communities, this custom is celebrated on 17th of Rajab on the assumption that Sayyidna Ali ﷺ was born on 11th of Rajab and the 17th of Rajab is the day on which his 'Aqiqa (Shaving of his head) was performed. In order to celebrate this happy event, the breads of some special type are prepared and after reciting Surah al-Mulk on them, they are distributed among the relatives and friends. This bread are generally called 'bread of Tabarak' because Surah al-Mulk is usually recited on them.

This practice is baseless because it is never proved that Sayyidna Ali ﷺ was born on 11th of Rajab or that his Aqiqa was performed on 17th of this month and, as explained earlier, even if these events are proved to have happened in those days, their commemoration through these specific rituals is not warranted by the Shari'ah.

## Conclusion

The above discussion indicate that the Shari'ah has not prescribed any specific way to observe the month of Rajab or to perform a specific mode of worship or a ritual in any one of its dates. However, being a prologue to the month of Ramadan, it should be availed of for preparing oneself for Ramadan and one should pray Allah to make him reach the blessed month and to benefit from its unique merits.

# Appendix 3

### Ahadith

Narrated by Ibn 'Abbas (Regarding the Verse) "And We granted the vision (Ascension to the heavens 'al-Mi'raj') which We showed you (O Muhammad as an actual eye witness) but as a trial for mankind" (17:60), Allah's Apostle 襁 actually saw with his own eyes the vision (all the things which were shown to him) on the night of his Night Journey to Jerusalem (and then to the heavens). The cursed tree which is mentioned in the Qur'an is the tree of al-Zaqqum.

[Sahih al-Bukhari, *Hadith* 8.610]

Narrated by Jabir ibn 'Abdullah The Prophet 襁 said, "When the Quraysh disbelieved me (concerning my Night Journey), I stood up in al-Hijr (the unroofed portion of the Ka'bah) and Allah displayed Bayt al-Maqdis before me, and I started to inform them (the Quraysh) about its signs while looking at it."

[Sahih al-Bukhari, *Hadith* 6.233]

Narrated by Abu Hurayrah: The Messenger of Allah 襁 said, "I found myself in al-Hijr and the Quraysh were asking me about my Night Journey. I was asked about things pertaining to Bayt al-Maqdis, which I could not preserve (in my mind). I was very much vexed, so vexed as I had never been before.

Then Allah ﷻ raised it (Bayt al-Maqdis) before my eyes. I looked towards it, and I gave them the information about whatever they questioned me. I also saw myself among the group of Prophets. I saw Musa saying a prayer and found him to be a well-built man as if he were a man of the tribe of Shanu'ah. I saw Jesus, son of Mary, (peace be upon him) offering prayer; of all men he had the closet resemblance to 'Urwah ibn Mas'ud al-Thaqafi. I saw Ibrahim (peace be upon him) offering prayer; he had the closet resemblance to your Companion (the Prophet ﷺ himself) amongst people. When the time of prayer came I led them. When I completed the prayer, someone said, 'Here is Malik, the keeper of the hellfire; give him salutation.' I turned to him, but he preceded me in giving salutation."

[Sahih Muslim, *Hadith* 328]

Narrated by Ibn 'Abbas: Regarding the Statement of Allah ﷻ "And We granted the vision (ascension to the heavens) which We made you see (as an actual eye witness) was only made as a trial for the people" (17:60), Ibn 'Abbas added, "The sights which Allah's Apostle was shown on the Night Journey when he was taken to Bayt al-Maqdis (i.e. Jerusalem) were actual sights, (not dreams). And the Cursed Tree (mentioned) in the Qur'an is the tree of al-Zaqqum (itself)."

[Sahih al-Bukhari, *Hadith* 5.228]

Narrated by 'Abbas ibn Malik: Malik ibn Sa'sa'ah said that Allah's Apostle described to them his Night Journey saying, "While I was lying in al-Hatim or al-Hijr, suddenly someone came to me and cut my body open from here to here." I asked al-Jarud who was by my side, "What does he mean?" He said, "It means from his throat to his pubic area," or said, "From the top of the chest." The Prophet further said, "He then took out my heart. Then a gold tray of Belief was brought to me and my heart was washed and was filled (with Belief) and then returned to its original place. Then a white animal which was smaller than a mule and bigger than a donkey was brought to me." (On this al-Jarud asked, "Was it the Buraq, O Abu Hamza?" He (i.e. Anas) replied in the affirmative.) The Prophet said, "The animal's step (was so wide that it) reached the farthest point within the reach of the animal's sight. I was carried on it, and Jibra'il set out with me till we reached the nearest heaven.

"When he asked for the gate to be opened, it was asked, 'Who is it?' Jibra'il answered, 'Jibra'il.' It was asked, 'Who is accompanying you?' Jibra'il replied, 'Muhammad.' It was asked, 'Has Muhammad been called?' Jibra'il replied in the affirmative. Then it was said, 'He is welcome. What an excellent visitor his is!' The gate was opened, and when I went over the first heaven, I saw Adam there. Jibra'il said (to me), 'This is your father, Adam; pay him your greetings.' So I greeted him and he returned the greeting to me and said, 'You are welcome, O pious son and pious Prophet.' Then Jibra'il ascended with me till we reached the second heaven. Jibra'il asked for the gate to be opened. It was asked, 'Who is it?' Jibra'il answered, 'Jibra'il.' It was asked, 'Who is accompanying you?' Jibra'il replied, 'Muhammad.' It was asked, 'Has he been called?' Jibra'il answered in the affirmative. Then it was said, 'He is welcome. What an excellent visitor his is!' The gate was opened.

"When I went over the second heaven, there I saw Yahya (John) and 'Isa (Jesus) who were cousins of each other. Jibra'il said (to me), 'These are John and Jesus; pay them your greetings.' So I greeted them and both of them returned my greetings to me and said, 'You are welcome, O pious brother and pious Prophet.' Then Jibra'il ascended with me to the third heaven and asked for its gate to be opened. It was asked, 'Who is it?' Jibra'il replied, 'Jibra'il.' It was asked, 'Who is accompanying you?' Jibra'il replied, 'Muhammad.' It was asked, 'Has he been called?' Jibra'il replied in the affirmative.

Then it was said, 'He is welcome, what an excellent visitor his is!' The gate was opened, and when I went over the third heaven there I saw Joseph. Jibra'il said (to me), 'This is Joseph; pay him your greetings.' So I greeted him and he returned the greeting to me and said, 'You are welcome, O pious brother and pious Prophet.' Then Jibra'il ascended with me to the fourth heaven and asked for its gate to be opened. It was asked, 'Who is it?' Jibra'il replied, 'Jibra'il.' It was asked, 'Who is accompanying you?' Jibra'il replied, 'Muhammad.' It was asked, 'Has he been called?' Jibra'il replied in the affirmative. Then it was said, 'He is welcome, what an excellent visitor his is!'

"The gate was opened, and when I went over the fourth heaven, there I saw Idris. Jibra'il said (to me), 'This is Idris; pay him your greetings.' So I greeted him and he returned the greeting to me and said, 'You are welcome, O pious brother and pious Prophet.' Then Jibra'il ascended with me to the fifth heaven and asked for its gate to be opened. It was asked, 'Who is it?' Jibra'il replied, 'Jibrail.' It was asked. 'Who is accompanying you?' Jibra'il replied, 'Muhammad.''It was asked, 'Has he been called?' Jibra'il replied in the affirmative. Then it was said, 'He is welcome, what an excellent visitor his is!' So when I went over the fifth heaven, there I saw Harun (Aaron), Jibra'il said, (to me), 'This is Aaron; pay him your greetings.' I greeted him and he returned the greeting to me and said, 'You are welcome, O pious brother and pious Prophet.' Then Jibra'il ascended with me to the sixth heaven and asked for its gate to be opened. It was asked, 'Who is it?' Jibra'il replied, 'Jibrail.' It was asked, 'Who is accompanying you?' Jibra'il replied, 'Muhammad.' It was asked, 'Has he been called?' Jibra'il replied in the affirmative. It was said, 'He is welcome. What an excellent visitor his is!'

"When I went (over the sixth heaven), there I saw Musa. Jibra'il said (to me),' This is Musa; pay him your greeting. So I greeted him and he returned the greetings to me and said, 'You are welcome, O pious brother and pious Prophet.' When

I left him (i.e. Musa) he wept. Someone asked him, 'What makes you weep?' Musa said, 'I weep because after me there has been sent (as a Prophet) a young man whose followers will enter Paradise in greater numbers than my followers.' Then Jibra'il ascended with me to the seventh heaven and asked for its gate to be opened. It was asked, 'Who is it?' Jibra'il replied, 'Jibra'il.' It was asked, 'Who is accompanying you?' Jibra'il replied, 'Muhammad.' It was asked, 'Has he been called?' Jibra'il replied in the affirmative. Then it was said, 'He is welcome. What an excellent visitor his is!'

"So when I went (over the seventh heaven), there I saw Ibrahim. Jibra'il said (to me), 'This is your father; pay your greetings to him.' So I greeted him and he returned the greetings to me and said, 'You are welcome, O pious son and pious Prophet.' Then I was made to ascend to Sidrat al-Muntaha (the Lote-tree of the Farthest Boundary). Behold! Its fruits were like the jars of Hajr (i.e. a place near Madinah) and its leaves were as big as the ears of elephants. Jibra'il said, 'This is the Lote-tree of the Farthest Boundary.' Behold! There ran four rivers; two were hidden and two were visible. I asked, 'What are these two kinds of rivers, O Jibra'il?' He replied, 'As for the hidden rivers, they are two rivers in Paradise and the visible rivers are the Nile and the Euphrates.'

"Then Bayt al-Ma'mur (the Oft-frequented House) was shown to me and a container full of wine and another full of milk and a third full of honey were brought to me. I took the milk. Jibra'il remarked, 'This is the Islamic religion which you and your followers are following.' Then the prayers were enjoined on me. They were fifty prayers a day. When I returned, I passed by Musa who asked (me), 'What have you been ordered to do?' I replied, 'I have been ordered to offer fifty prayers a day.' Musa said, 'Your followers cannot bear fifty prayers a day, and by Allah, I have tested people before you, and I have tried my level best with the Children of Israel (in vain). Go back to your Lord and ask for reduction to lessen your followers' burden.' So I went back, and Allah reduced ten prayers for me. Then again I came to Musa, but he repeated the same as he had said before. Then again I went back to Allah and He reduced ten more prayers. When I came back to Musa he said the same, I went back to Allah and He ordered me to observe ten prayers a day. When I came back to Musa, he repeated the same advice, so I went back to Allah and was ordered to observe five prayers a day.

"When I came back to Musa, he said, 'What have you been ordered?' I replied, 'I have been ordered to observe five prayers a day.' He said, 'Your followers cannot bear five prayers a day, and no doubt, I have got experience of the people before you, and I have tried my level best with the Children of Israel, so go back to your Lord and ask for reduction to lessen your followers' burden.' I said, 'I have requested so much of my Lord that I feel ashamed, but I am satisfied now and surrender to Allah's order.' When I left, I heard a voice saying, 'I have passed My order and have lessened the burden of My worshipers.'"

[Sahih al-Bukhari, *Hadith* 5.227]

Narrated by Malik ibn Sa'sa'ah: Allah's Apostle 攤 talked to his Companions about his Night Journey to the Heavens, when he reached the fifth Heaven, he met Harun. (Jibra'il said to the Prophet 攤), "This is Harun;; pay him your greetings" (The Prophet 攤 said,) "I greeted him and he returned the greeting saying, 'Welcome, O Pious Brother and Pious Prophet.'"

[Sahih al-Bukhari, *Hadith* 4.606]

Narrated by Anas ibn Malik: Allah's Messenger 攤 said, "I happened to pass by Musa (upon whom be peace) on the occasion of the Night Journey near the red mound (and found him) saying his prayer in his grave."

[Sahih Muslim, *Hadith* 5858]

Narrated by Ibn 'Abbas: The Prophet ﷺ said, "On the night of my Ascent to the Heaven, I saw Musa who was a tall brown curly-haired man as if he was one of the men of the Shanu'ah tribe; and I saw Jesus, a man of medium height and moderate complexion inclined to the red and white colours and of lank hair. I also saw Malik, the gate-keeper of the hellfire and al-Dajjal amongst the signs which Allah showed me." (The Prophet ﷺ then recited the Holy Verse), "So be not you in doubt of meeting him (when you met Musa during the night of al-Mi'raj over the heavens)" (32:23). Anas and Abu Bakr narrate from the Prophet ﷺ (that he said), "The angels will guard Madinah from al-Dajjal (who will not be able to enter the city of Madinah)."

[Sahih al-Bukhari, *Hadith* 4.462]

Narrated by 'Abdullah ibn Mas'ud: Allah's Apostle ﷺ said, "On the night of my Ascent (al-Mi'raj), I met Ibrahim and he said to me, 'Muhammad, convey my salam to your people and tell them that Paradise is a vast plain of pure soil and sweet water and that its trees cry, "Holy is Allah, all praise is due to Allah, there is none worthy of worship save Allah, and Allah is Great (*Subhana Llahi wa l-hamdu li Llahi wa la ilaha illa Llahu wa Llahu akbar*).""

[al-Tirmidhi, *Hadith* 1445]

# Notes

**Chapter 2**

1   The term "Aqabah' here does not refer to the pledge of al-'Aqabah which took place after the Night Journey, but to a place.
2   This was one of the leaders of Ta'if.
3   The two mountains of Makkah.
4   Salahi, M. A, *Muhammad: Man and Prophet* (Markfield: The Islamic Foundation, 2006), p.181.
5   Abdallah Marouf, Omar, 'The Preparation and Strategic Plan of the Propeht Muhammad for Islamic Jerusalem - A Critical Study of Muslim Sources .' PhD dissertation, University. Of Aberdeen, 2008, p.77.

**Chapter 4**

1   The semicircular space under the waterspout, that stands apart from the Ka'bah.
2   Al-Tabari, Tarikh al-Tabari, The History of al-Tabari, Albany State Uni. Of New York, 1992, Vol. xii. p.197.
3   The direction Muslims face when they perform the prayer (salah). Up until AH 2, Muslims faced Jerusalem and thereafter a revelation in the Qur'an called for a change of direction towards the Ka'bah in Makkah.
4   In the centre of the Noble Sanctuary lies a huge rock on which the Prophet 鸞 is assumed to have stood before making the ascension to the heavens. This entire Sanctuary was also the first qibla of the Muslims. At the end of the seventh century, the Umayyad caliph 'Abd al-Malik ibn Marwan ordered the construction of the Masjid over the rock. The construction became one of the most beautiful features of Jerusalem. Today the skyline of Jerusalem glitters with the golden Dome of the Rock, its most distinctive and famous landmark.
5   Al-Qurtubi, Muhammad ibn Ahmad, *al-Jami' li ahkam al-Qur'an* (Dar al Taqwa, Lndon, 2005)

6  Al-'Asqalani, Ibn Hajar, and Muhammad ibn Isma'il al-Bukhari, *Fath al-bari bi sharh Sahih al-Imam Abi 'Abdullah Muhammad ibn Isma'il al-Bukhari* [a commentary by 'Asqalani on the hadiths of Bukhari's *al-Jami' al-sahih*] (Beirut, 1989).

7  The place refers to the very first major fitnah that occurred regarding Prophethood; namely, that of Musaylima al-Kadhdhāb, who claimed Prophethood.

## Chapter 5

1  Sahih Muslim

2  Imam Ahmad

3  Sahih Muslim

4  A point in heaven superposed to the Ka'bah, and frequented daily by seventy thousand angels, each of whom never returns to it again until the Day of Judgment.

5  Sahih Muslim

6  A.I. Bulandshahri, *The Miracle of Mi'raj* (RedHill, South Africa, 1996), p.34.

7  Al-Bayhaqi

8  Sahih Muslim

9  "Al-Zarkashi (d. 794 AH / 1392 CE) (1998, (1) 197) argues that verse 45 of Chapter 43 of the Qur'an was actually revealed in IslamicJerusalem, during the Night Journey. The verse is as follows, "And ask the Messengers whom We sent before you, did We appoint any other gods, other than the Most Compassionate (i.e. Allah), that might be worshipped?" (43,45) Al-Suyuti quotes this narration, and also an addition by one of its narrators, al-Walid, who says that by 'al-Sham' the Prophet means 'IslamicJerusalem'. The researcher argues that this hadith is very weak because of the presence of 'Ufayr who is a very weak narrator as Abu Hatim al-Razi (d.327 AH / 940 CE) (1952, (7) 36) argues. Al-Razi actually specifies the narrations of 'Ufayr from Salim Ibn 'Amir from Abu Umamah, in particular, as being very weak and thus not at all reliable. In addition, this narration contradicts other strong opinions by scholars such as al-Zarkashi who says a number of verses were revealed in different places other than Makkah, Madınah and IslamicJerusalem, such as al-Juffah, al-Ta'if, and al-Kudaybiyah. The researcher argues that the mentioned h*adith* cannot be relied upon, despite its possibility [of]

being the only clue from the h*adith* of the Prophet Muhammad, due to its very weak status.

Many of the exegetes do not state whether or not this verse, verse (43,45), was revealed in IslamicJerusalem. Yet they mention two main opinions about the meaning of this verse. First is that, if this verse did actually occur, i.e. that the Prophet Muhammad was asked to ask the previous Prophets about this matter, it was revealed before or during the Night Journey. Second is that this verse is symbolic and did not actually take place. Exegetes such as al-Qurtubi (d. 671 AH / 1273 CE) and al-Alusi of the *Ra'y* School of *Tafsir*, support the first opinion. The majority of the scholars of the Mathir School of Tafsir do not specify this opinion, but do mention the different ones. Only al-Tabari clarifies his opinion after he points to the different narrations and opinions about this verse. He clearly rejects the first opinion, and supports the second. Also, one of the contemporary exegetes, Sayyid Qutb of the *Ra'y* School, supports the same opinion. Qutb argues that this verse is actually a metaphor that makes a strong impact on the reader of the Qur'an, by cancelling time, place, life and death, and draws a symbolic picture of the Prophet Muhammad questioning previous Prophets.

The researcher agrees with al-Tabari and Qutb. It is true that the verse directs the Prophet Muhammad to ask the previous Prophets about the presence of other gods. Yet this does not necessarily mean that this verse was revealed when he met the previous Prophets in reality during the Night Journey. It is unlikely that the Prophet Muhammad would have asked such a question to the previous Prophets, or even been ordered to ask in reality, since this could show that the Prophet may have had doubt about the monotheism of God and would have been ordered to ask the previous Prophets about that. The researcher argues that it seems that this is a metaphor that is used in logical discussion throughout the previous and later verses. The researcher actually doubts the arguments of the exegetes and the scholars of Qur'anic sciences, who say that this verse was revealed in Islamic Jerusalem. This argument is based only on a general look at the wording of the verse, not on any other valid evidence. It neglects the rhetorical structure of the verse and its coherence with verses before and after it" (Omar, Abdallah Marouf, The Preparation and Strategic Plan of the Propeht Muhammad for Islamic Jerusalem - A Critical Study of Muslim Sources,' PhD dissertation, University Of Aberdeen, 2008) p. 97.

## Chapter 6

1. al-'Asqalani, Ibn Hajar, and Muhammad ibn Isma'il al-Bukhari, *Fath al-bari bi sharh Sahih al-Imam Abi 'Abdullah Muhammad ibn Isma'il al-Bukhari* [a commentary by 'Asqalani on the hadiths of Bukhari's *al-Jami' al-sahih*] (Beirut, 1989), xvii. 258.
2. Sahih al-Bukhari
3. 'Some Notes on the Impact of the Story of the Miraj on Sufi Literature', *The Muslim World*, 63 (April 1973), 93.
4. Sahih al-Bukhari
5. Sahih al-Bukhari; narrated by Anas ibn Malik
6. Sahih al-Bukhari; narrated by Anas ibn Malik on the authority of Malik ibn Sa'sa'ah
7. Sahih al-Bukhari; narrated by Anas ibn Malik on the authority of Malik ibn Sa'sa'ah
8. Sahih al-Bukhari; narrated by Anas ibn Malik on the authority of Malik ibn Sa'sa'ah
9. Sahih al-Bukhari; narrated by Anas ibn Malik on the authority of Malik ibn Sa'sa'ah
10. Sahih al-Bukhari

## Chapter 7

1. Sahih al-Bukhari; narrated by Anas ibn Malik on the authority of Malik ibn Sa'sa'ah
2. Sheikh Muhammad ibn 'Alawi said, "The Prophet's greeting of Malik before Malik greeted him first agrees with the subsequent wording of more than one narrator whereby the Prophet said, 'I greeted him and he returned my greeting and welcomed me, but he did not smile at me,' and this is found in some of the narrations. However, the correct narration, as the compiler and others have said, is that it is Malik who greeted the Prophet first in order to dispel the harshness of his sight since his face showed severity and anger. It is possible to harmonize the two versions with the fact that the Prophet saw Malik more than once, so that Malik was first to greet the Prophet the first time, as we said, while the Prophet was first to greet Malik the second time, in order to dispel estrangement and to inspire familiarity. Know also that the Prophet's sight of Malik was not in the same form that those who are being punished see him."
3. Sahh Muslim
4. Imam Malik

5. Mishkat al-Masabih
6. Sunan Abu Dawud
7. Mishkat al-Masabih
8. Tirmidhi and Ibn Majah
9. "Ibn Hajar mentions that the account of the lady who combed the hair of Pharaoh's daughter is narrated from Ibn 'Abbas by Ahmad, al-Hakim, Ibn Hibban, and al-Bazzar, while Muslim in *Kitab al-zuhd wa al-raqa'iq* (#3005) mentions the part of the infant speaking to his mother before they are both thrown into the fire; and the mention of Yusuf's witness in verse 12:26 as being an infant is narrated from Ibn 'Abbas by Ibn Abu Hatim with a weak chain, and it is held by al-Hasan al-Basri and Sa'id ibn Jubayr. (It is also the explanation retained by Suyuti in *Tafsir al-Jalalayn*.) This brings the number of speaking infants alluded to in the hadith 'Those who spoke from the cradle are three' (Bukhari, Muslim, and Ahmad) up to five, and there are reports that increase it to seven or more; and Allah knows best" (al-'Asqalani, Ibn Hajar, and Muhammad ibn Isma'il al-Bukhari, *Fath al-bari bi sharh Sahih al-Imam Abi 'Abdullah Muhammad ibn Isma'il al-Bukhari* [a commentary by 'Asqalani on the hadiths of Bukhari's *al-Jami' al-sahih*] (Beirut, 1989), vi. 593–4).
10. Al-Tirmidhi
11. Ahmad
12. M.Shafi, *Maariful Qur'an* (Karachi: Publisher, 1996), i. 54.
13. Sahih Muslim
14. Sahih Muslim
15. Sahih Muslim
16. Sahih Muslim and al-Nasa'i
17. Sahih Muslim
18. Al-Nawawi

## Chapter 8

1. M. A. Salahi, *Muhammad: Man and Prophet* (Markfield: The Islamic Foundation, 2006), 184.
2. Ibid.
3. S. M. 'Alawi al-Maliki, *The Prophet's Night Journey and Heavenly Ascent* (Aqsa Publications, United Kingdom 2006), 37. (Originally from Ibn al-Qayyim's *Zad al-Ma'ad* and also cited by Ibn Hajar in *Fath al-bari*.)
4. S. Qutb, *In the Shade of the Qur'an*, trans. Adil Salahi (Markfield: The Islamic Foundation, 2005), xi. 187.

## Chapter 9

[1] Omar, Abdallah Marouf, 'The Preparation and Strategic Plan of the Propeht Muhammad for Islamic Jerusalem - A Critical Study of Muslim Sources .' PhD dissertation, University Of Aberdeen, 2008) p. 97.

## Appendix 1

[1] [Extracts from] al-Jaza'iri, 'Abd al-Rahman, *al-Fiqh 'ala al-madhahib al-arb 'a* [Islamic law according to the four schools] (Beirut: Dar al-fikr, 1960), i. 557.

[2] Muslim and Abu Dawud relate it in *Kitab al-sawm*, respectively in the "Chapter on Fasting at Times Other Than Ramadan", and in the "Chapter of Fasting During Rajab"; as does Ahmad in his *Musnad*.

[3] *Kitab al-siyam*, ("Chapter of Fasting During the Sacred Months"). Also found in Ibn Majah and Ahmad is the hadith of the man who repeats, "I can bear more," and to whom the Prophet 🕌 finally says, "Fast during the sacred months."

[4] al-Nawawi's commentary on, *Sahih Muslim*, Kitab 13 Bab 34 #179.

[5] Muslim relates it in the first chapter of *Kitab al-libas*, and Ibn Majah in the "Book of Fasting".

[6] *Ayyam al-tashriq* are the days of drying the meat after the sacrifice of Eid al-Adha: 11, 12, and 13 of Dhul Hijjah.

[7] Abu Dawud, *Kitab al-siyam* (Chapter 54); Bayhaqi, *al-Sunan al-kubra* 4,291; Suyuti, *al-Durr al-manthur* 3,235.

[8] There is also a Shiite scholar by the name of Muhammad ibn 'Ali ibn Babawayh al-Qummi (d. 380) who wrote *Fadai'l al-ashhur al-thalathah, 1. Shahr Rajab, 2. Shahr Sha'ban, 3. Sharh Ramadan* (Najaf, Matba'at al-adab, 1396/1976). Neither this volume nor hafiz al-Kattani's book on the merits of Rajab were available to us.

## Appendix 2

[1] T. Usmani, *Islamic Months* (Karachi: Ahmad Printing Corp, 1996), 49–63.

# Index

**N**
Nile (River), 35, 44, 45, 97

**O**
Ox, 51, 56

**P**
Pharaoh, 17, 51

**Q** ˙
Qiblah, 75
Qur'an, 7, 9, 10, 11, 12, 15, 27, 28, 43, 49, 64, 65, 72, 76, 77, 79, 87, 89, 93
Quraysh, 4, 12, 26, 69, 71, 73, 93

**R**
Rajab, 82
Razor, 55
Rocks, 47, 52, 54

**S**
Sa'd ibn Abi Waqqas, 33
Sahabah, 2, 23
Salaah, 50, 63, 91
Seed, 9, 38, 53
Shafi'i (Imam), 84
Stomach, 52
Sulayman Prophet (Soloman), 2, 13, 16-18, 39, 75
Surah al-A'raf, 16
Surah al-Anbiya', 17, 18
Surah al-Baqarah, 40, 65-68
Surah al-Isra', 8, 10, 20
Surah al-Tin, 76
Surah Saba', 18

Swimming, 43, 52
Syria, 15, 18, 51, 58, 61, 62

**T**
Tamim al-Dari, 33
Tawhid, 17, 23
Tirmidhi, 19, 29, 59, 62, 99

**U**
Umamah al-Bahili, 60
'Umar ibn al-Khattab, 2, 33, 83
Umm Salamah, 32
Ummah, 6, 12, 25, 32, 52, 53, 62, 68, 74, 75, 78, 89
'Umrah, 32, 91

**W**
Wood, 55

**Y**
Ya'qub Prophet (Jacob), 28, 77
Yusuf Prophet (Joseph), 35, 36

**Z**
Zaqqum (tree), 54, 72, 73, 93, 94
Zayd ibn Thabit, 19, 59